All the Clean Ones
Are Married

All the Clean Ones
Are Married

✳

AND OTHER EVERYDAY
CALAMITIES IN MOSCOW

LORI CIDYLO

Published in 2001 by
Academy Chicago Publishers
262 West Erie Street
Chicago, Illinois 60610

Printed and bound in the U.S.A.

Library of Congress Cataloging-in-Publication Data on file with
the publisher.

FOR MARIA,

AND FOR MY PARENTS,

WITH LOVE & GRATITUDE

CONTENTS

So What Do You Think of This Crazy Country?

ON A WINTER'S MORNING in 1991 I took my backpack and set out for Russia to become a freelance journalist. Everyone told me that my plan was foolhardy. "You're going to do *what*?" "It'll never work." "You don't even know anyone in Russia."

Who was I going to write for? Actually, I didn't know yet. Before I left I called the *New York Times*, the *Washington Post*, the *Chicago Tribune*, and a slew of other big newspapers. All the editors I spoke with, mostly crusty veterans in their sixties, curtly informed me that they had several full-time correspondents in Moscow and didn't need any freelancers. Get some experience, they said, and then maybe—in another ten years or so—we might have something to talk about. When an editor at the *Boston Herald* mentioned that the paper didn't have anyone based in Moscow, my pulse quickened with joy. But he wasn't very encouraging either. The *Boston Herald* was really a local paper, he told me: they just didn't do that much foreign news.

"Look, kid, I'd hate to see you go all the way to Russia for nothing. You may send us twenty good stories, and we may not buy any of them."

"All I'm asking for is a chance," I said.

An impatient sigh came from the other end of the line.

"All right," he said, "I'll take a look at whatever you send. But I can't guarantee anything."

Somehow I managed to squeeze a bit of hope out of that meager promise: the next day, I took all the money I had and bought a plane ticket to Moscow. At twenty-five I had the irrepressible optimism and fearlessness that only the young—or the foolish—have. I was afflicted (or blessed, depending on your point of view) with what Baudelaire called *gout du gouffre*, the "taste for the abyss."

It was the perfect time to go to Eastern Europe. Whenever I picked up a newspaper, it seemed that another democratic revolution had leveled yet another Communist regime. I had one thought: I should be *there*, not here.

"Here" was a small newspaper in Binghamton, New York, where the closest thing to crime was something locals called cow tipping (packs of teenage boys would roam the countryside and tip sleeping cows onto their backs, infuriating local farmers). My job was to ferret out the news—such as it was—in Broome County, and I often found myself in the town of Johnson City. It was the sort of place where the sheriff sits in an easy chair in front of a small color television, trimming his handlebar moustache while watching reruns of *Three's Company*. My first assignment was a front-page story about a mailman who refused to deliver the mail to a couple of houses because a dog owned by one of the residents had allegedly chased him, and he didn't want to risk another encounter with the beast. CANINE SUSPENDS DELIVERIES, the headline screamed. My editor sent a photographer to get a picture of the dog while I interviewed the mailman.

I had planned to stay at the *Press & Sun-Bulletin* for at least two years, but after nine months of stories like that one, I felt listless. The epiphany came when my editor sent me to Greene, another small town in the area, to watch a mule dive into a swimming pool. Local television camera crews swarmed around the pool as a stocky little man paraded an old, feeble-looking mule on a rein in front of a large crowd. The poor animal lumbered up the ramp to a twenty-foot-high diving board and stood there trembling. Finally it dived in. The little man grinned and bowed before the crowd. Everyone applauded except me.

The mule-diving act made the front page (with an action shot of the mule in midair, hooves flailing). As I stood by the edge of the pool that afternoon, looking at my soggy notebook—the mule had made a bigger splash than I had anticipated—I wondered: What am I doing with my life? Who in her right mind would drive sixty miles to watch a mule dive into a swimming pool and then drive *another* sixty to an office to write about it—and expect people to read it?

Then, suddenly and fortuitously, my editor mentioned that a group of Russian exchange students was flying in from Vladivostok that very evening. They were scheduled to arrive at 6:30. My shift ended at 6:00. Would I mind staying late to interview them and write up the story for tomorrow's paper? It would mean working a double shift, sixteen hours. I was in my car before he could finish explaining the assignment.

One of the students told me how much easier it was to be a journalist now that Mikhail Gorbachev was in power. Censorship had been all but eliminated. Another big change:

Russians were no longer afraid to talk to foreign journalists. "People are much more relaxed now," the student said. "Before, if they saw somebody with a notebook, they would run away or haul him into the nearest KGB office." As the students and I talked about glasnost and many other issues, I realized how much I enjoyed speaking Russian (I had studied it in college), and that evening, as I was driving back to the newsroom, I found myself thinking about the mailman and the mule, and about how much more exciting it would be to write about a country that was reinventing itself. A rogue thought entered my mind: Why not go to Russia and work as a journalist there?

When I first told my mother, who is Ukrainian and views Russians as heartless imperialists, that I was planning to move to Moscow to live there for a year or two, she burst into tears. "Moscow? But why? Why there of all places? What if there's another revolution? Do you want to die young? No," she said, sobbing so hard that she could hardly catch her breath. "I won't let you go!"

"Mom, I'm twenty-five," I said. But I knew that in her eyes I was still her *ribcha*, which means "little fish" in Ukrainian. The day I moved to Binghamton, which is about two hundred miles from Yonkers, where I grew up and where my parents still live, she stood by the door, crying. "It's so far away," she said plaintively. And now here I was, telling her that I would be leaving for Russia. We were standing by the kitchen window in my parents' Victorian house, but I had the impression that she didn't see the oak trees, the Hudson River, or the pink-and-orange sky, made golden by the setting sun. She was somewhere else, it was obvious.

"We'll still see each other," I said, taking her hand in both of mine. "I'll come to Yonkers, and you can visit me in Moscow."

"No," she said softly, "I'm not going there. It's better if you come here."

"Why?"

"I'm sick of Communism."

"But, Ma, you'd be going there to see me."

She never did come to visit me. I suppose she must have been thinking of ghosts. I understood her anguish. I felt both drawn to Russia and repelled by it at the same time. But I always knew that I would go there someday. It was just a question of when.

*   *   *

My parents never talked about the past. "What does it matter?" my mother would say. "We live here now."

But the past *did* matter, at least to me. As a child I begged my parents to tell me something—*anything*—about my ancestors, but they always evaded my questions.

Then one night we were driving down a dark country road in Connecticut, and suddenly my father started talking. For eighteen years, he had been silent on the subject. Now, sitting contentedly in the passenger seat, he couldn't stop chattering. Maybe it was the wine. Or maybe it was because he had nothing better to do. Normally my father did the driving; that night my brother, Peter, was behind the wheel. Somewhere along the way Peter had turned left instead of right, and now we were lost. My father, who drove a cab for many years, has a keen sense of direction, but he had forgotten to bring his glasses, so there was nothing for him to do but sit back and relax while Peter tried to figure out which narrow dirt road would take us back to I-95.

"You kids don't realize how easy you have it," my father said in his heavy Ukrainian accent. "When your mother and I were growing up, life was hard. We had to stand on line for hours just to get a new pair of shoes or a winter coat. Remember how it was, Hania?"

"Oh, shush," my mother snapped. For he was shouting. It wasn't that he was angry, that's just the way he speaks, a by-product of having been raised on a farm, my mother says. What does shouting all the time have to do with being a farmer? "Your father and his family worked in the fields all day. One person might be planting corn at one end, and another one might be tilling the soil all the way on the other side. They had to call out across the fields: 'Hey, Kostek, it's time to feed the pigs!' He got used to yelling." As my father rambled on in his stentorian voice, she grimaced and said, "This is what happens when you marry a country boy." My father ignored her and kept right on talking.

I found out that five of my cousins perished during Stalin's brutal collectivization campaign. They had lived in Poland all their lives, but in 1932 they emigrated to the Ukraine, believing that it was their duty to join the proletarian revolution in their homeland. They were buoyed by idealism and the promise of jobs, free housing, and medical care for all who dared to follow the difficult but heroic path to a bright Communist future. Altogether nine people—three women and six children—all from Werchovna Wielka, a small southern village, made the journey.

When they arrived in rural Ukraine, there was no housing for them or any of the other new immigrants, many of them also from Poland. People were living in barns, abandoned shacks, or out in the fields. The collectivization of farms had begun. Hundreds of thousands of kulaks, well-to-do peasants, were forced to surrender their land and livestock, often at gunpoint. Those who refused were "liquidated"—either shot or sent to a concentration camp. By 1933 more than a million peasants had been killed or imprisoned. The few who managed to survive, mostly poor peasants and "proletarian revolutionaries from brother countries," such as my relatives, were forced to work on enormous collective farms run by incompetent, often drunk directors who allowed tons of grain to rot.

Food was becoming increasingly scarce; people were fainting in the fields. Then one day the workers learned that a new law had been passed: they were not to be given any grain until the Five-Year Plan had been fulfilled. A few Ukrainian officials tried to explain to the Kremlin leadership that such a policy would lead to mass starvation. Stalin sentenced them all to death by firing squad.

Watchtowers manned by armed guards stood in the fields, and anyone caught stealing grain was shot. Even children, some as young as three or four, were summarily executed.

Dead horses and cows were everywhere, and wild-eyed dogs roamed the streets. People ate whatever they could catch and kill: dogs, cats, birds, mice, rats. . . . Some slaughtered their friends and neighbors; a few even devoured their own children. Those in the final stages of starvation lay in their huts, slowly dying. Every day special brigades collected all the new corpses and threw them into mass graves. (Western historians estimate that five to seven million Ukrainians starved to death during what became known as the Great Famine of 1932–33.) Meanwhile people had to march and sing and carry red banners bearing such slogans as WE THANK THE COMMUNIST PARTY FOR OUR HAPPY AND PROSPEROUS LIFE!

One of my cousins tried to escape, but Stalin demanded absolute loyalty from his subjects: once you entered the Soviet Union, you were a citizen for life. She was shot by Soviet border guards and died somewhere on the Russian-Polish border.

My father suspects that another of my cousins, who mysteriously disappeared—and then resurfaced in Moscow—was working for the KGB. "How could a poor village boy just pick up and move to Moscow?" he wonders. "His mother was always so secretive. She wouldn't tell me anything about him, not even his address."

Moving from a small Ukrainian village to Moscow in the fifties was suspicious indeed. Even now one cannot move to any of the more desirable urban centers, such as Moscow or St. Petersburg, without a *propiska*, a residence permit, which can only be obtained by marrying someone who has one (my cousin was single), through bribery (his family didn't have that kind of money), or through well-placed "friends." Anyone who agreed to work for the KGB would surely have been granted one.

His mother had tried to return to Poland. She spent the last of her savings on fake passports for herself and her three children—the ones they had were destroyed by customs officials when they entered the Soviet Union—but they were turned away at the border. With no money and no place to go, they were forced to live in the forest. Luckily it was spring, and they managed to survive on berries, roots, grass, leaves, and bark. Three months went by. Finally, by some miracle, the Soviet authorities allowed her to exchange the house she had left behind in Poland for a small house in the Ukraine. (She and her other two children, who are now in their seventies, still live there.)

No one in the family knows what became of the others. Like so many other Ukrainians, they probably died of starvation.

In those days mail sent abroad from the Soviet Union was heavily censored. The letters my cousins sent my grandparents were sporadic and eventually stopped altogether. My grandparents assumed that they were just too busy to write. They did not learn of their tragic fate until many years later.

In fact, my grandparents had nearly become Soviet citizens themselves. In 1946 Jan and Varvara Cidylo were living on a small farm in Werchovna Wielka with their four children: two boys, Konstantin and Piotr (my father), and two girls, Maria and Anna. My father, the second oldest, was thirteen.

News traveled fast in the countryside, and word soon reached Werchovna Wielka that there were job opportunities in the Soviet Union. Having lost twenty-seven million people to World War II, Stalin was once again promising free housing, health care, and a secure future to anyone who came. Enticed by this image of prosperity, and eager to rejoin her relatives in the Ukraine, my grandmother served my grandfather his usual breakfast of goat's milk and porridge one morning and told him she wanted to emigrate.

The window of their little log cabin was open. The sun had just come up, and the warm summer air smelled of flowering plum trees. A rooster crowed, and in the distance a wizened shepherd, holding a wooden staff, tended to his sheep. My grandfather, who had a long grizzled beard and red sun-baked skin, put down his spoon and listened to his wife's pleas. He was not shocked—he knew very well that she missed her family—merely surprised. A taciturn man who liked to think things over before venturing an opinion, he rose from the table, put on his black cap, and headed for the door, promising my grandmother that they would talk about it later. He had no idea that she had already applied for visas.

After he fed the chickens and milked the cow, he spotted a young Russian soldier leaning against a cherry tree, smoking a cigarette. Taking off his cap, my grandfather shook hands with the soldier and asked him if there was any truth to Stalin's lavish promises. Would he and his family have a better life in the Soviet Union?

The soldier tossed his hand-rolled cigarette to the ground and crushed it with his black boot. He looked at my grandfather long and hard. My grandfather could see that he was trying to decide whether he should tell him the truth. They stood there, eyeing one another in the morning sunlight. It was the soldier who finally broke the silence.

"You are a farmer?

"That's right.

"You have livestock, then?

"I have five pigs, a goat, a cow, and some chickens.

"What will you do with them if you go?

"Well, I thought I might sell them to my neighbor—he has a farm just up the road—and use the money to buy a few animals once I get settled in the Ukraine."

"If you do that, you'll be branded a kulak, and they'll take everything away from you."

"And what will I get in return?"

The soldier let out a sour laugh. "Nothing. And they will probably kill you and your family besides."

"I see," my grandfather quavered. "Thank you . . . for telling me the truth." He started to walk away, but the soldier put a menacing hand on his shoulder, looked him straight in the eye, and said, "If you tell anyone what I just told you, I'll kill you."

My grandfather understood that the soldier had threatened him merely to protect himself—if anyone had found out about what he had told my grandfather, he would have been executed or sent to a labor camp.

When my grandfather came home that evening, he told my grandmother what the soldier said and warned her not to tell anyone in the village. "Ach, what nonsense!" she scoffed. "You don't even know that boy. Why do you trust him so?" But my grandfather, who must have made quite a ruckus when he found out about the visas, ordered her to withdraw the applications. She did, and they stayed on their farm in Werchovna Wielka.

That year there was another famine in the Ukraine, and the murderous collectivization campaign began afresh.

I wish I knew more than these meager facts, but they are all that my father remembers of the story my grandfather told him. (I know almost nothing about my mother's family.)

I have often wondered what would have happened to my father had fortune arranged things a little differently in 1946. Had my grandmother held the deciding vote, the family would have emigrated to the Ukraine. Would they have survived the famine? The collectivization campaign?

I suspect that for my father such questions are too painful to contemplate. Yet, as the months passed while I waited for my visa, it was he who persuaded my mother to accept my decision. "Let her go," he said. "You see how stubborn she is."

When I arrived in Moscow, Russia was undergoing its most dramatic transformation since the 1917 Bolshevik Revolution. Three months had passed since the failed Communist coup against Gorbachev. The coup plotters had been led away in handcuffs, the Communist Party was in ruins, and for the first time, no one—not even those "above," as Russians say— had any idea where the country was headed. Everyone was on tenterhooks of suspense, wondering what would happen next.

Such was the atmosphere when I started my new job in the English-language department of what was then known as TASS (the Telegraphic Agency of the Soviet Union). I had signed on as a *stilist* (literally, a "stylist"), a sort of bilingual copy editor. It didn't pay much—four hundred dollars a month plus some rubles—but it did entitle me to a work visa, which meant that I could stay in Moscow for a year (had I gone on a tourist visa, I would have been allowed to stay for only a month). My plan was to work full-time at TASS and write freelance stories for American and European newspapers whenever I could. After my one-year contract with TASS was up, I would devote all my time to writing—I was sure that all those editors who had so blithely dismissed me when I called from New York would change their minds. But that was in the future. At the moment I was to edit news dispatches (sent by TASS correspondents based in various countries) and translate Gorbachev's speeches and decrees from Russian into English. I had just turned on my computer and was still trying to get used to the sight of a Cyrillic keyboard when a tall, wiry young man approached my desk. He smiled shyly, revealing two dimples. "You must be Lori," he said. "My name's Sasha. I'm a translator here. So what do you think of this crazy country?" I laughed, but I soon realized that Sasha wasn't being facetious. Two weeks after I arrived, the Soviet Union collapsed.

On that bone-chilling December night, Russian president Boris Yeltsin and the leaders of Ukraine and Belorussia (now Belarus) met secretly at a secluded forest lodge in Viskuoi, somewhere near the Belorussian city of Brest. Television cameras moved in for a close-up of Yeltsin as he came out of the lodge. Speaking on behalf of the group, he summarily announced the dissolution of the Soviet Union and declared that a new, loose association, made up of eleven of the fifteen republics, would take its place. They had decided to call it the "Commonwealth of Independent States" (CIS) ; there was no mention of the four republics that had refused to join the new union. Within hours, an enraged Gorbachev pronounced the move "illegal," and a hastily assembled panel of judges and law professors was shown sitting around a conference table, debating whether the country could be dissolved by three people.

I stood in front of the television at TASS, watching it all with Matvei, an editor who worked on the international desk. "This is another coup," he said. "How can three guys get together and decide that a country no longer exists? Could three of your governors go off to the Hamptons for a couple of days and then announce to the world that the United States doesn't exist anymore?"

Sadruzhestvo Nezavisimikh Gosudarstv (SNG), the Commonwealth of Independent States, sounds terrible in Russian. The acronym requires the speaker to utter a deep, guttural *g*, and does not roll off the tongue easily. You really can't say it too many times in the same sentence without sounding ridiculous, and it wasn't long before people started making fun of it. Even smooth television anchors looked embarrassed as they fumbled with the new name during the evening news. Some newscasters deftly sidestepped the issue by simply saying, "our country."

But how the new name sounded wasn't its only shortcoming. Since the three Baltic states (Latvia, Lithuania, and Estonia) and Georgia had opted out, you couldn't use it to refer to the entire country unless you wanted to say "SNG, plus the Baltic states and Georgia." Try saying that more than once in the same sentence! In everyday conversation people were more likely to say, "whatever this country is called now."

After a week or so, somebody came up with "the former Soviet Union." Pretty lame, I thought. But people had to call it *something*. Obviously we couldn't go on living in a country without a name. Or could we?

One evening I came home from work and carried the television into the kitchen so that I could watch *Vremya*, the state-controlled evening news, while I fixed dinner. A reporter, an earnest-looking young man in horn-rimmed glasses, was traveling around the country asking people on the streets a simple question, "What country do you live in?" Judging by the looks on most people's faces, you would think that he had asked them to name the first five American presidents. "The Soviet Union," a few answered. Others just stood there, their breath forming little constellations of vapor in the cold. "What country do I live in?" asked one man, repeating the reporter. After a long pause, he smiled sheepishly and said, "That's a good question."

On December 25, 1991, just two weeks after the Commonwealth of Independent States was created, Gorbachev stepped down as the last leader of the Soviet empire. Sounding sad and defeated, he said in his final televised speech, "My life's work has been accomplished. I have done all I could." Moments later he signed over the nuclear missile–launching codes to Yeltsin, his archrival and successor. At 7:32 p.m., under the silver glow of the stars, the red flag of the Soviet Union was lowered for the last time.

That night, Lyudmila, one of my colleagues, came running into the newsroom and handed me a story. At the top someone had written SROCHNOYE, "urgent." Quickly I corrected a few grammatical mistakes. Then I stumbled across the words "Soviet Union." I looked at the clock on the wall: 7:45. The country had been dead only thirteen minutes.

Should I cross out "Soviet Union?" But what would I change it to? I couldn't write "the Commonwealth of Independent States." Since the story clearly referred to the entire country, that wouldn't be accurate. I considered changing it to "the former Soviet Union," but that sounded too ethereal. I knew that Lyudmila would be back any second. SROCHNOYE, I had learned, meant five to ten minutes. I also knew that newspaper editors and television producers, who were doubtless wondering how they should refer to the Soviet Union now that it no longer existed, would soon be calling us—in those days TASS was the official Soviet news agency, the mouthpiece of the government. What would I tell them? How could I, an American, decide what this country should be called?

I took the elevator to the tenth floor and knocked on my boss's door. "*Zakhodite*. Come in," said a gruff voice. Sitting behind a massive oak desk, puffing on a cigar, was Aleksandr Sergeyevich Nechayev, the head of the English language department. A brilliant linguist (he spoke fluent English, Chinese, and Italian) with a penchant for vodka and dirty jokes, he was often in a foul mood. Judging from the expression on his face, it looked as though tonight was no exception.

"*Govorite*. Speak," he muttered.

"I need some guidance," I said, handing him the story I had been editing. "Take a look at the second line. What should I do?"

He studied the story for a moment, then blew three smoke rings into the air. They hovered above my head as I sat in a brown leather armchair opposite him. "I really don't know what to suggest," he said. "There is no Soviet Union as of," he looked at his watch, "twenty-five minutes ago. So where are we living? Who the hell knows? That's the least of our problems."

"Hasn't this issue been discussed at editorial meetings?" (It had been obvious for weeks that historians would soon be writing about the Soviet Union in the past tense.)

Nechayev laughed acidly, as if to say, *Silly girl.* TASS, he reminded me, didn't have enough pens (we had to bring them from home) or paper (we printed out on both sides). And had I forgotten the nights that we hadn't been able to send any news over the wire because we had run out of printer ribbons? Did I really think that anyone had the time to worry about the name of the country? Besides, he fulminated, stubbing out his cigar and gesticulating with both hands, the situation was so volatile that there wasn't much point in coming up with an editorial policy. Who could tell what might happen tomorrow? There could be a civil war.

He took off his glasses, rubbed his eyes, and said, "Put whatever you want."

I changed it to "the former Soviet Union." It sounded awkward, but it would have to do.

A couple of British newspaper editors and a Swedish television producer called. I told them I wasn't sure what the country's new name was. They were astonished.

When my shift ended at 1:30 that morning, I put on my coat, turned off the lights, and took the elevator down to the lobby. There on the wall was a large blood-red star and a gilt hammer and sickle, the symbols of the Bolshevik Revolution. I used to look at them every morning while I waited for the elevator. I wondered how much longer they would be there. Nechayev had been right about one thing: a civil war was not out of the question. With Russia's history of violent upheavals, anything was possible. I was beginning to feel nervous.

Into the cold I went. At this hour there were almost no cars on the road, and I was the only person standing on the curb, waiting for the trolleybus. By the time I got home it was 2:30, but somehow I wasn't tired. Without taking off my coat, I went into the living room. On the wall was an enormous map of the Soviet Union. There, in big, widely spaced Cyrillic letters that seemed to float over the republics were the words everyone had thought were immutable: SOVIET UNION. I imagined the pale yellow, pink, and brown chunks of land vanishing into the aquamarine ocean—one-sixth of the world's landmass gone without a trace. Cartographers will be busy soon, I thought.

The next day Nadia, a translator, said half-jokingly: "Maybe our jobs are like the Soviet Union, a mere illusion; maybe they'll disappear soon too. Pouf!" She snapped her fingers: "Just like in *The Master and Margarita*." A few of us laughed at this reference to Bulgakov's satire of life in the USSR. A couple of days later, Nechayev strode into the office and asked everyone to stop what they were doing. "I have an announcement," he said. Nechayev looked as though he hadn't slept all night. He was wearing the same red shirt he had worn the day before; under his eyes there were dark, puffy pouches. He took a deep drag of his cigarette and exhaled through both nostrils. For a moment he stood with his eyes downcast, as though he wasn't sure how to begin. "We might all lose our jobs," he said finally. A hush fell over the room, the hum of the computers the only sound. "We don't know who we're working for anymore. Officially we're still the Telegraphic Agency of the Soviet Union, but there is no Soviet Union. How can we go on working for a country that doesn't exist?"

A man's voice came from the back of the room: "Respected Aleksandr Sergeyevich, can you tell us how much time . . . when we can expect. . . ."

"We may close next week or six months from now. We just don't know."

A couple of women, who were in their fifties, cried softly. They had been with TASS all their lives.

As for me, I wondered how I would do without a Communist-era perk to which I had grown accustomed: virtually free housing. My monthly rent was five hundred rubles—the equivalent of one dollar. Back then it was customary for large state enterprises to provide their employees with apartments, and I had been granted a spacious three-room *kvartira* with a toilet that worked (most of the time, anyway). I had no idea where I would go if TASS went the way of the Soviet Union. Newspapers didn't carry apartment listings because there was no rental market, at least not officially. The only way to find a place was through connections, and I didn't have any.

That same week Nechayev told me and the other two stylists, who were also American, that TASS had no American dollars—as foreigners we were supposed to receive half our salaries in dollars and the other half in rubles. (The Russians in the department were paid only in rubles.) The money, he explained, was "tied up" in Vneshekonombank, the state-run bank in which all enterprises were required to deposit their foreign currency earnings. (The bank had been in the headlines the previous week. It had gone belly-up, and its spokesman had declared that all accounts would be frozen indefinitely, creating large-scale panic, particularly among foreign companies, many of which lost millions of dollars.) I listened, wide-eyed, as Nechayev told us that from now on we would receive only the ruble portion of our salaries. Just five weeks before, I had been comfortably ensconced in New York, reading about Russia's economic crisis in the newspapers. Now it was cutting into my paycheck.

To our disbelief TASS insisted that we sign new contracts. They were placed on our desks one morning by a dapper man named Vladimir Ilyich Novikov. With the same first name and patronymic as Lenin, it seemed fitting that Novikov, the "secretary" at TASS, whom I referred to as the Senior Coffee Drinker, had the kind of makework job the Soviet Union was built on. Whenever I asked for him, his assistant gave the same reply: "He's in the cafeteria taking a coffee break." After a while I went directly to the cafeteria and usually found him there. That morning I spotted the Senior Coffee Drinker sitting at a table in the corner, over by the pastry cart. The table was near a window, and his gold watch caught the sunlight as he buttered a roll and plopped two small cubes of sugar into his coffee. Bemused, I asked him what the point was of signing a new contract when the old one had been violated so cavalierly. He took a bite of his roll and explained, quite seriously, that *this* contract was "binding" and that I should return it to him by the end of the week so that he could put it in my file.

I knew that it would be impossible to live on the ruble portion of my salary—all the Russians at TASS did translations *na levo*, "under the table," for dollars. I thought maybe I could earn some money this way too. But when I asked a few people how they managed to find such work, they just smiled and whispered, "Through friends."

I was bending over the bathtub, washing some heavy sweaters, when I heard Yeltsin's familiar baritone on the evening news. Quickly I grabbed a towel to dry my hands and rushed into the living room. Speaking in solemn tones about "the painful road ahead," Yeltsin announced that prices on all consumer goods would be freed from state controls—literally overnight—and that they would rise significantly. He asked his fellow Russians to be brave and patient. It would be a long time, he said frankly, before their lives would change for the better. The economic experiment was to begin on January 1, 1992.

It was impossible to tell exactly how much prices would go up or whether the plan would work. But one thing Yeltsin said was clear enough: the centrally planned economy had failed miserably. It was December 1991, yet the country looked as if it was still recovering from World War II. There were shortages of everything: vegetables, fruit, cheese, eggs, milk, sugar, even bread. People spent hours every day foraging for food. Finding a decent cut of meat was like finding a five-hundred-ruble note on the street. It didn't happen often, and you felt incredibly lucky when it did. More often than not people came to work with bad breath and greasy hair, not because they didn't care how they looked or smelled, but because they didn't have any choice—soap, toothpaste, and shampoo were available only on the black market for American dollars.

News bulletins about the latest shortages were announced like sports scores on the radio. I remember waking up one morning and hearing that there was enough meat in Moscow to last nineteen days, enough butter for forty days, and enough eggs to last something like thirty days. With each broadcast the numbers got lower. It was hard not to feel frightened.

Women took turns buying groceries for one another during their lunch hours and talked about all the delicious dishes they would make if only the ingredients were available. In those days, no matter whose apartment you went to, dinner was always the same: fried beef cutlet, fried potatoes, and a small salad of tomatoes, cucumbers, and radishes, smothered with mayonnaise. Everyone served the same thing simply because there was nothing else.

It's amazing how your tastes change when there are so few choices. I had never eaten radishes before, and at first they were about as flavorful as cardboard. But the more I ate them (almost every day), the more I learned to tolerate their papery taste and eventually, I even began to like them.

Even now I can't forget the terror of that first day of "economic reform." Goods were plentiful, but prices had risen beyond the bounds of anyone's imagination. Russian television showed two *babushki* sobbing in front of a meat case. "We're going to starve!" one of them wailed after picking up a package of sausages and looking at the price. The sausages, which the *babushka* could have bought only the day before for 1 ruble and 25 kopecks, now cost 195 rubles. Her monthly pension was 125 rubles.

Exotic fruits that few Russians had ever seen—bananas, kiwis, mangoes, and pineapples—suddenly appeared on every street corner. I once saw an elderly couple staring at a box of kiwis as one might stare at a glittering green rock from Jupiter. "What do you think those are?" the woman asked the man in a whisper. "I don't know," he whispered back. "I think monkeys eat them in Africa." Although they were eager to try one of the strange, fuzzy little fruits, they soon abandoned the idea when the vendor named his price: 1,500 rubles (about $15.00) a kilogram.

Most people in the West didn't seem to understand why so many Russians were against the "liberalization of prices," as the government called its new economic program. Western newspapers tended to cast such people as diehard Communists who still believed that the economy could be revitalized through more efficient central planning. But their opposition had nothing to do with ideology. How would we Americans feel if the price of a gallon of milk suddenly rose from $1.50 to $300.00? Would we be willing to pay that much simply because the president assured us that it was the way to economic recovery?

Like the *babushka* in the meat shop, many people were impoverished overnight by the new reforms, their life savings reduced to the equivalent of a few pennies. A couple of days after the most daring economic experiment of modern times began, I was standing in front of my apartment building, a dreary high-rise in southwest Moscow, trying to get a taxi. It was one o'clock in the afternoon, and already it was getting dark. Snowflakes the size of cotton balls were cascading from the gray sky, and a mighty gust of wind snatched a few people's hats from their heads. High into the air the fur hats soared, sending their owners running. Having forgotten my own hat, I put on my hood and stood there shivering as dozens of mud-spattered cars drove past me, ignoring my outstretched hand. Finally one stopped. I negotiated a price and was already sitting in the front seat when a woman tapped on the window with a gloved hand. With her was a girl of seven or eight. The driver rolled down the window and asked the woman where she was headed. Kutuzovsky Prospekt, she answered, and handed him some money.

The driver gaped at her. "You expect me to take you all the way downtown for five hundred rubles?

"Please, I'm a helpless widow with a child. Five hundred rubles is all I can afford. Would you be so kind—"

"I need to live," the driver said gruffly.

"And I can't offer you more because I need to live too," she replied tearfully.

The driver thought for a moment, then told the woman to get in. Her face brightened instantly, and she and the little girl slid inside. As she brushed the snow from her boots, the woman launched into a diatribe on the new economic policy, and she and the driver developed an instant rapport, the way that strangers who share a common hardship often do. She nodded sympathetically as he explained that he had to moonlight as a cabdriver on evenings and weekends because his job as a surgeon no longer paid enough to make ends meet. "If only one could draw rubles and use them to buy things," the woman said wearily. They went on in this vein, talking about how miserable life was, for some time. Finally the driver turned to the woman and said, with bitter irony, "Why don't we go hang ourselves?" I was stunned.

A few weeks later, I asked Nechayev if I could take some time off to fly to New York for my friend Annemarie's wedding. "When is it?" he mumbled, without looking up from the stack of papers on his desk.

"March 25," I replied.

He raised his head. "But that's a month away. If we're still alive then, yes, you can have a few days off."

I usually don't remember much from works I've read, but that afternoon, I recalled a scene from Chekhov's *Uncle Vanya*. One of the characters steps out onto the veranda and says, "What a lovely day!" Uncle Vanya, a prototypical Russian, replies, "It would even be pleasant to go hang oneself on a day like this." Apparently, I thought, Chekhov had not exaggerated the fatalistic nature of Russians.

Yet, in those early days of economic experimentation, a certain degree of fatalism was understandable, perhaps even inevitable. Politicians, who often sounded as if they were following a lab manual, seemed to have only the haziest notion of what they were aiming for. A "market with a specific Russian character" sounded like another vague, well-worn oxymoron, "socialism with a human face," and we all knew what had come of that. As *U.S. News & World Report*'s Doug Stanglin put it, "I think they make it up as they go along." I felt more than a little pessimistic myself as I watched my monthly salary (eight hundred rubles) shrink to nothing. More than three times the average wage when I arrived in November, by February it was just enough to buy two kilograms of potatoes, three kilograms of oranges, one kilogram of cucumbers, and a loaf of black bread.

Desperately afraid that citizens might riot, the government had to find a way to make the massive price rises more palatable. And so it was that capitalism, the emblem of the decadent West, suddenly became the focus of a Soviet-style public relations campaign. "We are going toward a market economy," a voice on the television at TASS boomed one day, with the self-congratulatory air of the old record-breaking harvest reports. "I don't believe it," said one of my colleagues in disgust. "It sounds just like the propaganda they used to feed us in the old days, except now they're telling us that we're 'going toward' a market economy." She rolled her eyes as the omniscient voice assured viewers of a happy ending ("We will all be more prosperous"), just as it had in the past.

One often had that eerie feeling of déjà-vu. Yeltsin still used the language of a Party man (quite simply because it was the only one he knew—he *was*, after all, a Party man). Whenever I heard him speak, I imagined an aide retrieving one of Leonid Brezhnev's old speeches from the Kremlin archives and going through it carefully, crossing out the words "Communism" and "socialism" and neatly penciling in "democracy."

On television the revolution that swept through Russia in 1991 looked marvelous. Masses chanted and knocked down monuments; a new flag was raised. People hugged one another and cried tears of joy. This rapid sequence of events made it seem as though everything had changed. At least, that appeared to be the general perception in the West. The reality as I experienced it was that in many ways, things stayed the same.

"So, how fast is the mail in the new Russia?" an American newspaper editor once asked me. He was astonished when I told him that the mail in the "new Russia" was just as slow as it had been in the old Soviet Union. Did he imagine that all the sullen, lazy postal clerks in the country had been fired and replaced by cheerful, efficient workers who get the mail out on time?

Actually, in Moscow's Central Post Office, there are still just two clerks in charge of sorting mail from abroad and only one of them can read English (I read this in a Russian newspaper). Imagine two people sorting mail for a city of ten million! At last I understood why letters from home took months to arrive—if they arrived at all. The article also noted that two bags of mail from overseas had been found at the bottom of the Moscow River. The reporter didn't mention how they got there. I wondered if those two overworked clerks had anything to do with it. Perhaps they had decided, while taking a coffee break one afternoon, that they were fed up with trying to sort mail for ten million people.

This is how I imagine it: from the window, the one just above the electrical outlet where they plug in the coffeepot, the women could see the Moscow River. Surveying the mountains of unsorted mail, they resolved to go down to the river that very evening with as many sacks as they could carry. But the sacks were heavy, so they each took just one. The guard, who was suspicious when he saw the women dragging two bulging postal sacks, gave them the once-over. "We went grocery shopping on our lunch hour," one of the women blurted out. The guard knew that she was lying; he also knew that he would get an earful if he said anything. So he let them pass. "A typical man!" one of the women would have said if the guard had dared to question their story. "And just what do you *think* is in the bags? Six kilograms of potatoes, that's what. We have families to feed, and there's no time to shop after work. Excuse me, but you men don't lift a finger. Everything is up to us: the cooking, the cleaning, the shopping. . . ." And so it was that two bags of mail from abroad ended up in the Moscow River.

Many other aspects of daily life seemed similarly impervious to change. One of the things that surprised me the most when I first arrived in Moscow was the public bathrooms. Wherever one went—to restaurants, theaters, movie houses, coffee shops, train and bus stations—none of the toilets had seats, which made using them difficult if not impossible for women (one had to be particularly agile). I don't recall ever having seen toilet paper or soap in a public bathroom either. To make matters worse, the toilets didn't flush (the water just swirled around a little), and there were often pieces of bloody cotton on the bottom—probably the reason the toilets didn't work. Those bits of bloody cotton meant that women still didn't have sanitary napkins or tampons. Obviously, I thought, Communism wasn't working, at least not for women.

Just before I left Russia for good, in 1997, I went to TASS to say good-bye to Sasha. Though I had quit my job as a stylist in 1992, the guards—whose military-style uniforms still bore the Soviet hammer and sickle—remembered me and let me pass. I asked one of them for the key to the bathroom. Opening the door, I saw that there were still no toilet seats. No toilet tissue either, just cut up pieces of newspaper in a filthy plastic bin that had once been white. Needless to say, there was no soap. The pieces of bloody cotton were still there too. By then both sanitary napkins and tampons were available, but many women couldn't afford them and continued to use wads of cotton, gauze, or bits of old towels. So for them, in that sense, nothing had changed. I washed my hands with cold water (there was no hot water in the building), dried them with a tissue from my handbag, and walked back to the lobby. As I sat on a soft green couch, waiting for Sasha, I recalled the question he asked me on my very first day at TASS: "So what do you think of this crazy country?"

It occurred to me that Russia was as unstable as ever. Although the days of high inflation were over, people's wages had never really recovered. Six years after Yeltsin's radical economic reforms, a quarter of the population was living below the poverty line. As for the political situation, one still had the feeling that anything could happen at any moment. Every August, while American newspapers are filled with lighthearted fare about Labor Day weekend getaways, Russian newspapers abound with dark predictions of another coup. (This trend began after the coup against Gorbachev in August 1991. The first rumblings of the October 1993 coup, officially known as "an armed rebellion," also began in August, thus permanently marking that month as a supremely unlucky one in many people's minds.)

"If only we lived in a normal country," is a refrain that is often repeated. For some reason—even with the trappings of democracy—Russia never quite achieves that modicum of normality, that ordinariness, even dullness, that Russians crave.

Imagine a presidential candidate stepping up to the rostrum and promising voters that he won't send anyone to a labor camp. That's exactly what Gennadi Zyuganov, the Communist candidate, told his constituents when he ran for office in 2000. Then there was the public opinion poll, conducted the same year, that attempted to gauge how Russians envisioned their future. The following choices were given as possible answers to a question about what might happen should Zyuganov be elected president:

1. Expect a Communist dictatorship.
2. Expect the restoration of censorship.
3. Expect the restoration of socialism.
4. Expect a civil war.

Will Russia ever become a "normal country?"

At the moment it's hard to imagine. Russians are (to borrow a phrase, used in a different context, by the Hungarian political observer György Konrád) "the complainers intoxicated by failure." Even buttoned-down newscasters seem to take a perverse pride in the outlandishness of post-Soviet life; they often weave irreverent sallies about their country into the news. One well-known television anchor (who, ironically, was later appointed Yeltsin's spokesman) once quipped before reading an item on the evening news, "And now, something that could happen only in our country . . ."

This Way to the Russian Federation

AMBLING DOWN SOVIET ARMY STREET one apricot-colored summer afternoon, I spotted a pink neon sign. ALL FOR YOU, the cursive letters flashed in English; a purple fluorescent arrow pointed to a staircase. I walked down three narrow steps and opened the massive door. The hinges creaked, and when I let go, the door slammed shut. I found myself inside a ramshackle shop that smelled like an old broom closet. A fine sepia-colored film covered the shelves, and cobwebs hung from the ceiling. In the corner was a tiny window; motes of dust whirled in the small patch of sunlight. I marveled at the motley array of goods: laptop computers, teddybears, refrigerators, lacy underwear, icons, Elvis posters, a pink bathtub with golden lion-paw feet, and a green-and-red parrot in a bell-shaped cage. "*Ty mnye nadoyela!* I'm sick of you!" the parrot squalled.

I wanted a television set. A black-and-white model would do. My eyes scanned the shop. There, next to a giant poster of the King in a studded jumpsuit, was a small black-and-white Zunabirov, and it cost only five hundred thousand rubles, the equivalent of one hundred dollars. All the other shops I had been to sold only Japanese color televisions for one million rubles (two hundred dollars). Even when I chanced upon a *skitka*, a sale, they went for at least eight hundred thousand rubles (one hundred sixty dollars).

Did anyone work in this place? "*Alyo!*" I called out. All I heard was the echo of my own voice. Maybe the sales person had stepped out. Then I noticed a bell on the counter. Next to it was a sign: PLEASE RING FOR ATTENDANT. I rang. No response. I tried again. A stout old woman with a moustache and a few dark hairs sprouting from one of her chins shuffled out of a back room. She was holding a cup of tea in one hand and a cucumber in the other. She looked at me with obvious irritation. "*Da?*" I asked her whether the TV came with a warranty. Three creases formed on her brow. "A *what?*" When I explained the concept, she cackled. "Oh, no," she said, still laughing, "we don't have anything like that."

I bought the TV anyway. The following evening, I was watching *Carried Away by Wild Horses*, a Soviet made-for-TV movie about an urban woman who falls in love with a Cossack. Resplendent in an embroidered peasant blouse, a silver saber tucked into his billowing blue pants, the hero was showing his new love, a sheltered scientist, how to ride a horse bareback. The two of them were galloping through the countryside, her long blond hair pushed from her smiling face by the wind. Suddenly a snake slithered out from behind a tree. The woman's horse neighed and reared; a scream echoed through the countryside: onto the ground the woman fell, hitting her head on a rock. The hero leaped from his horse and slew the snake with one powerful sweep of his saber. Just as he was bending over the heroine's limp body, the picture dissolved into horizontal black lines. Lifting the side panel, I tinkered with a few knobs. The lines were still there, only now they were vertical. When I switched channels, the TV hissed and crackled so loudly that I was afraid it might explode. Finally I turned it off and called a repairman. When he arrived the next morning, I was in a hurry and tried to direct his attention to the TV, but he seemed much more interested in my coffee table. Made of dark cherry oak, its legs were elegantly curved, and each side was shaped like the top of a heart. "What a funny-looking table," he said. "Did you bring it from America?"

"No," I told him. "I bought it here."

His eyebrows arched in surprise. "Well, I guess they're making different kinds of furniture now." He fixed his gaze on the table again and shook his head. "It's too weird for my taste. I like our standard Soviet coffee tables better."

(The repairman was unable to fix the TV, so I decided to use it as a radio. Only the sound worked. As for the images that were supposed to accompany the words, I had to use my imagination.)

Later that same week, I called Lyudmila to invite her to a dinner party at my apartment. Just before I hung up, I said, "Don't forget to bring my copy of *Lady Chatterley's Lover*." A gifted translator with an impressive command of English, Lyudmila could quote whole sections of Lawrence, Faulkner, and Hemingway and discuss their works knowledgeably. She didn't look the part of a Russian intellectual, though. She didn't wear old, moth-eaten sweaters or drab, shapeless dresses; she always looked well rested; and I don't believe I ever saw a cigarette dangling from her glossy red lips. Tall and lanky, with frizzy brown hair, which she permed herself, Lyudmila dressed in the exaggerated feminine style that Russian women often prefer. Though I had told her that the party would be an intimate affair, Lyudmila arrived in a shimmering evening gown, and as she made her way into the dining room, she swayed her hips a little, Mae West–style. *Clickety-clack, clickety-clack*, went her red high heels as she sashayed across my parquet floor. She walked toward my bookcase, holding *Lady Chatterley's Lover* in one dainty, well-manicured hand. The sound of her shoes stopped abruptly; Lyudmila was standing in the middle of the room, staring at the coffee table.

"Where did you get this table?"

"Russkiy Suvenir."

"It's beautiful," she said, touching the smooth, polished surface. "It reminds me of a table I saw in an American movie once, I forget what it was called. That actress—the one with the long hair and the big teeth—what's her name? Julia Roberts. She was in it."

Lyudmila told me that when she first started watching American films, in the early 1990s, she was fascinated by the variety of furniture. Here was a dreamland of seemingly endless possibilities, so many different kinds of desks, chairs, lamps, and coffee tables, such a profusion of colors and styles. It was actually possible to buy the kind of furniture one liked, to *choose*.

Her eyes, which were accustomed to seeing the world through a prism of Soviet uniformity, couldn't help noticing something else: not only was the furniture different in each film, it was displayed in various ways. Lyudmila was especially captivated by the couches. "I remember I was watching *Fatal Attraction*, and there was this scene—Glenn Close and Michael Douglas were on a couch, kissing and ripping each other's clothes off—and I thought, Now, how can they do that? How can they put a couch in the middle of the room? It would look terrible. Then they showed them from the back and I noticed that the couch was actually finished—it was completely covered with fabric, not just in the front, like ours.

I too had the standard Soviet couch. Or, rather, my landlord did. He and his family had lived in the apartment before I moved in, and their furniture was still there. When I first noticed that the couch was backless—all you could see was cheap wood—I assumed that it was defective. Maybe he bought it at a discount place, I thought. Then I noticed that everyone's couch was like that.

Nowadays upscale shops sell imported couches *with* backs. Along with Western-style supermarkets, cafés, and restaurants, such shops are infusing the stark, utilitarian landscape with a splash of color. With their neon signs and fanciful, sometimes awkward-sounding names, such as ALL FOR YOU, BURGERS ON THE RUN, and CHIC YOU WILL SOON BE, they are giving some streets and neighborhoods a more distinctive character. In Soviet times grocery stores, cafés, bakeries, and hair salons were all standardized. And instead of names—perish the bourgeois notion—the Communists gave them plain-vanilla labels: CLOTHING, SHOES, BAKERY, RESTAURANT, CAFÉ. One city looked just like another. One neighborhood, street, or apartment building was indistinguishable from the next.

In the classic Soviet-era film, *Irony of Fate*, Zhenya, a Muscovite, ends up in someone else's apartment in St. Petersburg (then Leningrad) and doesn't realize it because the street, the building, and even the inside of the apartment all look exactly like his own. His key even fits the lock.

The night before Zhenya's wedding, he is celebrating his last hours of bachelor freedom with three close friends and six bottles of vodka. After the many toasts of the evening have worked their magic, Zhenya's buddies—who don't want him to get married—whisk him off to the airport and deposit him in a plane bound for St. Petersburg. Zhenya stumbles off the plane and takes a taxi "home." Staggering into the apartment, he takes off his pants and passes out on the floor. Nadia, the woman who lives in the apartment, opens the door and screams: there is Zhenya, sprawled next to the dining room table, snoring like a chain saw. Grabbing Zhenya by the shoulders, Nadia shakes him and slaps his face. "Who are you?" she shrieks, "and what are you doing here?" Zhenya mutters something, then goes back to sleep. Furious, Nadia fills a pitcher with cold water and pours it on Zhenya's head. He wakes up instantly. Still hung over, he slips and falls a couple of times as he tries to stand up. Finally he grabs the edge of the table and hoists himself up. Pushing his wet hair out of his eyes, he growls at Nadia, "Who are you? And how did you get into my apartment?"

Just then the door opens. In saunters Nadia's lover, clutching a bouquet of red roses. Seeing Zhenya, who is clad only in a shirt and boxer shorts, he throws the roses down on the floor. "So *this* is how it is, eh?" Nadia tries to explain. "Don't insult me even more with your lies!" he sneers. "And you—" He takes a step toward Zhenya. "Do you know who I am? *I* am a respected member of the Communist Party. Don't think that there won't be consequences!"

Later he takes Zhenya aside and says calmly, "Let's suppose that you really do live in Apartment 12, Building 25, Third Builder's Street in Moscow, and that your friends really did put you, who were in a drunken state, on a plane to Leningrad. When you opened the door, didn't you notice that the furniture was different?"

"But the furniture is the same!"

"All right, let us accept for the moment your contention that the furniture *is* the same. Didn't you notice that the apartment is being repaired?"

"But mine is being repaired too!"

Marina, a friend of mine who has a keen eye for the farcical side of Soviet culture, still howls with laughter every time she watches that movie, which is shown on TV every New Year's Eve. One year I watched it with her. We were curled up on my couch, under a fluffy blanket, sipping tea with honey. The movie had just ended, and Marina was reminiscing. "Oh, how we lived in those days! Whenever you invited someone over for the first time, it was impossible to explain what your building looked like because all the other buildings in the neighborhood looked just like it. Usually I would stand in front of the door and yell, 'Over here!'" As the final credits scrolled down the screen, Marina told me a story that Andrei Myagkov, the actor who made a name for himself playing Zhenya, had recounted in a television interview.

One day a friend invited Myagkov to his apartment. Since the friend had to work late, he told Myagkov that he would leave the key in the mailbox and that he should let himself in and wait. "Just make yourself comfortable, I'll be there in a half hour or so," the friend said.

Myagkov found the key and opened the door. To help pass the time, he turned on the TV. Nothing but smiling peasants driving combines through perfect-looking

wheatfields. ("In twenty years, the Soviet Union will sur-
pass the United States in the production of wheat and many
other commodities. . . .") Noticing a bottle of cognac in the
liquor cabinet, Myagkov got up and poured some into a
snifter.

The hunger pangs in his stomach were getting harder to
ignore. If only he had something to snack on. Pickles went
well with cognac; maybe his friend had some. He went into
the kitchen and opened the refrigerator. On the top shelf,
behind a pot of borscht, was a big jar of *ogurtsi*. He took
the jar back into the living room, put his feet up on the
standard coffee table, and feasted on the pickles. Every so
often he got up to pour himself some more cognac. Glancing at the window, Myagkov noticed that it was getting dark.
He began to wonder where his friend could be. Maybe something had come up at work. He was a publisher, after all,
and deadlines were tight. Or, maybe—he was reluctant even
to consider such a possibility—his friend's car had skidded
on the icy road and . . . Well, why sit here, imagining the
worst? Taking out his address book, he found his friend's
work number and called him.

"Where are you, old boy? I've been waiting for two
hours. I've already helped myself to some cognac and—"

"Cognac?" asked his startled friend. "But I don't have
any cognac."

Myagkov hung up the phone, washed the snifter, put
the cognac, the pickles, and the key back where he had found
them, and ran out of the apartment.

I, too, often got lost in the maze of identical apartment buildings. It was 4:30 one afternoon, and a bunch of us were

standing in front of the TASS building, waiting for the tram. I had just finished working the early shift—which began at 7:00 in the morning—and I was tired. When the creaky, mud-caked tram finally came, I was grateful to find a seat. Wiping a corner of the dusty window with my glove, I soon spotted a cluster of bleak, prefabricated concrete buildings that looked just like the ones on my street. I pulled the cord by the window; a buzzer sounded. The doors opened, and I bounded out into the snow only to discover, from the name-plate, that this was Heroes of the Revolution Boulevard, not Kulakova Boulevard. I turned around just in time to see the doors closing. Moving with astonishing speed, the tram chugged down a steep hill and disappeared from view. Down the hill I ran, but my fur boots were heavy, and the snow was knee deep. . . . Panting, I finally caught up with the tram. I knocked furiously on the door, but I had mittens on—and a pair of gloves underneath—and the sound got muffled. (The driver, who was staring straight ahead, couldn't see me.) Using my teeth I tore off my right mitten, then the glove—but, before I could knock again, the light changed and the tram went hurtling toward the next stop.

A sturdy-looking woman in a brown astrakhan coat and a beaver-skin hat walked past me. "*Izvinitye*," I said. "Can you tell me where Kulakova Boulevard is?"

"Don't know, can't help you," she said, without breaking her stride. It was only five o'clock, but the sky was already black, and there was no moon, and I had no idea where I was. I stood there in my enormous fur boots, looking at the dozens of identical apartment buildings, wondering what to do. The silence was broken only by the sound of the wind, which swept the glittering snow up into the cold air.

I scanned the buildings on the other side of the street, hoping to find a nameplate. But from that distance I couldn't see anything, even with my glasses. I would have to get closer. Like many Moscow streets, the one I was standing on was fourteen lanes wide; attempting to cross it would be like trying to walk across the Long Island Expressway. The only safe way to get to the other side was by going through a large underground tunnel. I looked for the familiar blue sign and spotted it on the corner: PEREKHOD ["Underpass"], it read. Gingerly I made my way down the slick, icy stairs and entered the tunnel.

The damp, chill air reeked of urine and rotten cabbage. The ground was wet, and the sickly glow of the fluorescent lights made the puddles look green. I put my hands into my pockets and walked briskly; shards of broken glass crunched under my boots. Suddenly I heard footsteps behind me— heavy, rapid, and unmistakably male. I quickened my pace. So did the man; the heavy thud of his footsteps grew louder and echoed in the tunnel. I searched frantically for an exit, but I couldn't see very far ahead of me, and the footsteps were getting closer . . .

"I've caught up with you at last," said a deep male voice. I found myself face-to-face with a muscular man who towered over me. He was at least six feet tall and dark skinned. His black hair was disheveled, his face pockmarked. He stared at me with his small dark eyes. Outside, a light rain was falling; a cold drop fell from the dirty, cavelike ceiling and slid slowly down my cheek. In his right hand, the man was holding a pair of shiny black gloves. He put them on, slowly and deliberately. First one glove, then the other. Without taking his eyes off my face, he reached into his coat

pocket . . . I knew that I should do something—run, scream—
but all I could do was watch that hand in its shiny black
glove. The man grinned weirdly, and pulled out—a crumpled
white handkerchief. "You certainly do walk fast," he said
offhandedly. And then, suddenly angry: "You were *trying*
to get away from me." He wiped the sweat from his brow
and put the handkerchief back into his pocket. Was he toy-
ing with me? "It's not safe for a young lady to be out all by
herself at night," he said, grinning. "There are a lot of mani-
acs out there who would really enjoy a nice young thing like
you." (He emphasized the word "enjoy" in a way that made
my skin crawl.) "You be careful now." And then he van-
ished as suddenly as he had appeared.

I didn't know what to make of this bizarre episode. Had
the man meant to attack me and then changed his mind? Or
did he just enjoy scaring people?

As my heart rate returned to normal, I suddenly realized
how vulnerable I was, a woman, young and alone in a foreign country. Unlike many Russian women, who carry Mace
or some other kind of weapon, I had nothing. What would
I have done if the man had tried to strangle or rape me?

As I climbed the steps that led out of the tunnel, I wondered if anyone had ever considered the dangers of stan-
dardization. If it were possible to distinguish one street from
another, I wouldn't have gotten lost and would never have
ended up in a dark tunnel with a lunatic. I was just beginning to understand what a disorienting place Russia can be.

Walking along the boulevard, I came to a drab concrete high-
rise. Was *this* my building? There was no nameplate, so I
went inside. The rusty mailboxes looked the same. So did

the broken elevator. And the stench—created by urine, booze, and cigarettes—was certainly the same. A dulcet ballad blasted from a big black boombox: "We met in the cold, cold tundra, dancing to the beat of the stars/The earth was frozen, but your body was warm,/Do you want me still, my Siberian love?"

Sitting on the landing was a teenage girl in a bubble-gum-pink sweater and black leggings. She was singing along as she applied a nail polish that was the same color as her sweater. Another girl, a Madonna look-alike with a big silver cross around her neck, was bumping and grinding to the beat; her fashionably tousled blond hair fell into her eyes as she wiggled her hips. I asked them if this was Kulakova Boulevard. No, said the one who was dancing, this was Workers' Paradise Street. She stopped for a moment to turn up the volume on the radio, then went back to her bump-and-grind routine.

How was I ever going to find my way home?

Shambling through another underpass, I was fortunate enough to come across a drunk. Drunks are everywhere in Russia, slumped over in the doorways of decaying buildings, stumbling onto trams and buses, and here, in the underground world of *perekhodi*. Ordinarily I steered clear of them, but this particular drunk was selling lightbulbs, something I needed desperately. A lightbulb in a state store would have cost me fifty rubles, but I hadn't been able to find any in more than a month, so I was willing to pay the four hundred rubles the drunk was asking. There was just one problem: I wasn't sure what wattage I needed. "Don't you worry," he said. "These are the right ones, all right."

"How can you be so sure?" I asked.

He opened his soiled blue knapsack, revealing dozens of lightbulbs, a few rolls of toilet paper, and a bottle of cheap vodka in a brown paper bag. Pushing a lock of pumpkin-colored hair off his pale forehead, he reached into the knapsack and fished out a couple of lightbulbs. "Which room are they for?" he asked, slurring his words and swaying a little.

"The living room. I have a lamp in there."

The drunk rubbed the pumpkiny stubble on his chin. "Well," said he, leaning against the grimy wall to steady himself, "if they're for the living room, then they're definitely the right kind. Lightbulbs for living room lamps are all the same. They're standard."

I imagined all the lamps in the country casting an identical glow from identical lightbulbs. A little eerie. Then again, this was a society that craved uniformity even in thought. Nikolai Bukharin, a member of Lenin's inner circle, had talked of mass-producing "standardized" socialist intellectuals, "as if in a factory." If human beings could be standardized, why not lightbulbs?

I plunked down eight hundred rubles for the lightbulbs and asked the drunk if he knew where Kulakova Boulevard was. He tore off a small piece of his crumpled paper bag, took a stubby pencil out of his pocket, and drew a map. "*Vot*," he said, pointing to a little square box he had drawn, complete with door and chimney. "This is your street. From here it shouldn't take you more than fifteen, maybe twenty minutes." Exhausted but heartened, I thanked the drunk and set out for Kulakova Boulevard, following the arrows on my tiny map.

When I finally found my apartment, I went back outside and took a good look at the building. There had to be *something* distinctive about it. When I looked carefully, I saw that someone had smashed a hole in the plastic panel on the front door. But then I noticed that the doors of three of the other buildings had holes too. So I memorized the shape of the hole—it looked a little like a horse's hoof-and made a mental note that it was just above the doorknob. And that was how I learned to recognize my building, by looking for the horse's hoof.

That was in 1991. Getting around town is even more difficult these days. The Soviet Union is gone, but the identical buildings are still there, and now the names of nearly all the major streets and squares have been changed. Even cities have been renamed. Gorky is now Nizhny Novgorod, Zagorsk has become Sergeiv Posad, and Boris Yeltsin's hometown of Sverdlovsk has reverted to its prerevolutionary name, Yekaterinburg.

The hoopla before those cities were stripped of their Communist-era monikers—stories in all the major newspapers, reports on television, radio announcements. If only someone had told us which streets and squares were going to be renamed . . .

It was a midsummer day in 1997, and the air was suffocatingly hot. I didn't mind, though. In Russia it's cold for most of the year, from September until May. Sometimes even the summers are chilly. Once—in the middle of June—it snowed.

So, that afternoon, when the temperature climbed to 38 degrees Celsius (98 degrees Fahrenheit), I tossed my fur boots, which looked like two scraggly terriers, into the closet and pulled out a pair of sandals. I was supposed to meet a friend inside the Kitai Gorod ("China City") metro station, but I didn't know where it was, and I had only twenty minutes to get there. I ran outside and signaled to oncoming cars with my right hand. A dusty green Zhiguli came to a sputtering stop. Behind the wheel was an old woman wearing dark sunglasses and, of all things, an LA Dodgers cap.

"*Kuda?* Where to?" she asked.

"Kitai Gorod metro station. Know where that is?"

"Can't say I do, but we'll find it."

The woman unlocked the door, and I slipped into the front seat.

Glancing in the rearview mirror, she tucked a few wisps of auburn hair into her cap. "Right now I look terrible," she remarked, "but when I fix my hair and put on some makeup, I look *vot tak*," and she gave herself the thumbs-up.

"I don't mind telling you," she went on in a confidential tone, "that my husband is *much* younger than I am—fourteen years, to be precise. In this country, that's a scandal.

"But he married me for love," she said dreamily. "I don't have my own apartment or anything. There *are* men who prefer older women. They like to be taken care of, to be well fed, and above all, to be praised. Our women are so much better educated than men! But a good wife knows how to make her man feel that he is stronger and wiser than she. Men are such fragile creatures. . . . Where did you say you were going?"

Her name was Yekaterina, and she told me that she was a retired maid of Brezhnev's. "He ran around a lot," she said of the doddering former Soviet leader. "I remember his first mistress, a Tatar with slanted eyes. She liked jewelry, that one. He used to buy her diamond necklaces, sapphire earrings. . . . Leonid Ilyich wasn't much of a husband, that's for sure. But he wasn't a bad man to work for. There were always little presents on holidays, and he gave me time off whenever I needed it."

But Yekaterina's pension wasn't enough to live on, so she picked up passengers like me a few times a week to earn extra money.

In the twenty minutes that we had been on the road, we saw many metro stations, but not the one we were looking for.

"Where can it be?" Yekaterina muttered, as we drove past a flashing red neon Coca-Cola sign. She pulled a map out of her glove compartment, took a quick look, then stuffed it back inside. "It's no good. It's from 1996."

I checked my color-coded metro map, which I had bought only the week before. No China City.

"Never mind," she said. "We'll ask that militiaman over there." She pulled over abruptly. As she was getting out of the car, two men behind us honked and jeered. "Oh, go shoot yourself!" Yekaterina yelled. "Just *what* is so interesting?"

But the men merely laughed and drove away.

The militiaman had no idea where the elusive metro station could be. "How should I know?" he said. "I'm from Irkutsk."

When Yekaterina got back into the car, her cheeks were flushed. "This country is so backward," she raged, as she turned on the ignition. "Those idiots back there! In America probably no one pays any attention when they see a woman behind the wheel. It's considered normal, right?"

Yes, I said, it was common to see women driving. I had a license myself.

I told Yekaterina about the time I heard a popular Russian radio personality say (on the air) that women were "biologically incapable" of driving and that they shouldn't be allowed to apply for a license. "Honestly, I think it's dangerous for women to drive," the broadcaster, a woman who had her own late-night call-in show, had said. "They're so easily distracted. Suppose a woman has to pass a shoe store. She may spot the perfect pair of pumps to go with that elegant little skirt—and crash headlong into the car in front of her."

"That's just the sort of brainwashing that we're up against," Yekaterina fulminated. "And the women are even worse than the men! My own daughter doesn't approve of me driving. Only my mother-in-law understands me, but she was raised in a different time. . . ."

We were approaching a busy intersection. Traffic was heavy, and a few cars drove up onto the sidewalk.

No, I thought, she *wouldn't*.

She did.

As we careered across the sidewalk, I heard a swishing sound and then a crackle, as though something had just snapped. When I opened my eyes, there were some leaves and a couple of twigs on the windshield. Slowing down, Yekaterina brushed away the foliage with one hand, then stepped on the gas pedal, propelling the little black needle on the speedometer to one hundred twenty k.p.h. [about 85 m.p.h.].

Up ahead a stooped-over *babushka* was coming out of a bakery, clutching a loaf of bread in a plastic bag. "Maybe the old lady knows something," Yekaterina said hopefully. And she hit the brakes, bringing the Zhiguli to a screeching stop. Surely, I thought, as I let go of the dashboard, there must be a less hazardous way of getting to China City.

"I've lived in this neighborhood all my life, and I've never heard of such a street," the *babushka* told us. "It must be one of those new ones. What's the old name? Do you know?"

We had been driving around for almost an hour and were just about ready to give up when another passerby told us that China City was actually Nogin Square. "The devil take those democrats!" Yekaterina fumed as she turned the car around. "The country is falling apart, and they're sitting on their asses, making up new street names!"

It all started with a few side streets in early 1992. Hardly anyone noticed. Then the momentum began to pick up, and by 1993 it became impossible *not* to notice. Clandestine meetings were held, and an entire country was redesigned by a group of balding bureaucrats in ill-fitting polyester suits and slightly tinted plastic glasses, the kind that were popular during the Soviet era and are still in vogue among apparatchiks. I imagine them huddled over a long, burnished conference table—every bureaucrat's office still has one—poring over a giant map of what is now known as the Russian Federation. A junior-level bureaucrat, a young man who still has all his hair and does not yet wear the requisite glasses, stands there with a notebook, dutifully recording the hundreds of new names his superiors have come up with in a concerted effort to make citizens' already complicated lives even more difficult.

The problem with the new addresses is that many of them exist only in those bureaucrats' notebooks. Often a street is renamed, but the old nameplate is still on the building and the new one hasn't been put up yet. Some streets have no name at all. There, on the facade, is a faint trace of the old nameplate, a spot where the paint is slightly darker, slightly cleaner. Someone has removed it, but in its place is—nothing. Walking down such a street is like reading an anonymous poem. No matter how lovely it is, it leaves you feeling a bit bereft.

When people give their address, they usually write down two: the old one and the new one. But sometimes they forget to give both street names, and you forget to ask. Of course, once you leave your apartment and enter the labyrinth, it's too late—since most pay phones don't work, there is no way to reach the person. Given all the confusion over the new names, though, it's perfectly acceptable to be late for a dinner party, a doctor's appointment, or even a job interview. I'm ashamed to admit it, but I'm almost always late, no matter *what* country I'm in. So for me, Russia's (or, rather, the Russian Federation's) ever-changing cartography conferred an unexpected advantage: however late I was, I had a credible excuse.

Some of the new names irked me. I was walking along Ulitsa Gertsena one morning when I noticed that the bureaucrats had put up a new sign. I stared at the strange new name: Ulitsa Bolshaya Nikitskaya. *What was wrong with Ulitsa Gertsena?* I wanted to ask one of those bureaucrats. That street was my favorite part of Moscow, and I had hoped that it might be spared.

Most streets bore the twin signatures of the Soviet era: crumbling concrete buildings and dimly lit courtyards strewn with garbage. With its elegant prerevolutionary mansions, old-fashioned lampposts, and neatly trimmed lilac trees, Ulitsa Gertsena harked back to the days of horse-drawn carriages and the grand nobility of Pushkin's time. Walking along its winding pathways, I imagined slim-waisted women in diamond tiaras and white gloves walking alongside moustachioed men in black top hats. I loved to stroll past the sumptuous manors. With their pale pink, yellow, and green facades, they looked like holiday cakes. Sometimes I would follow the stone path that led to the Moscow Conservatory, Russia's top music academy and one of the finest in the world (Serge Rachmaninoff, Emil Gilels, and Mstislav Rostropovich all studied there). In front of the academy was a large flowering tree that bloomed in summer. I would stand underneath it and listen to the soft strains of Bach, Handel, or Tchaikovsky while its delicate white petals fell all around me. I felt especially lucky when I chanced to hear Beethoven's last piano sonata (No. 32) or Mozart's *Magic Flute* Overture. Through a small window I could see the young pianists, their eyes closed in deep concentration as their fingers glided over the keys.

For me the serene beauty of the conservatory was part of Ulitsa Gertsena, not some newly invented street called Bolshaya Nikitskaya. Standing in front of the shiny new sign that day, I think I understood why so many of my Russian friends still call St. Petersburg by its Soviet name, Leningrad. It isn't that they yearn for the old order. In fact, they were overjoyed when Russia finally severed itself from Communism. Using the old name gives them a sense of continuity, a modicum of stability in their tempestuous lives.

But the renaming of streets, squares, cities, and the country itself has raised another issue. As one Russian friend put it, "People think that because Communism was bad, it's right to destroy everything that was associated with it. But the old names are part of our history. How can we destroy our own history?"

On the embankment outside the Central House of Artists, a museum in Moscow, there was once a graveyard of fallen idols. They had been toppled from their pedestals during the frenzy of the 1991 coup. Lenin, Marx, Engels— they were all there, sprawled ignominiously on the grass. Many of them were missing an arm or a leg; a few had been decapitated. They were there because someone thought that it was important for people to remember, for parents to show their children the relics of the brutal system they once lived under.

One summer evening, when the sky was orange, I went there and discovered that the past had been neatly swept away. Only three years had passed since the coup, and already all those famous body parts had been removed, stashed away in some giant warehouse where no one will ever find them. As I looked at the emptiness all around me, the soft grass still bearing the giant footprints of one of the statues, I thought about my Russian friends and felt a pang of sadness. The czarist past had been extirpated from history and from memory because it threatened the Communists' power. Now the democrats were obliterating all the symbols of the Communist past in an effort to consolidate their own power.

Every day another monument is destroyed, another street, another square renamed, in the hope that soon—

within a generation or two—people will forget, which is exactly what will happen. Already my friend Lena's nine-year-old son, Grisha, is asking her, "*Mama, kto Lenin?*" Lena, a historian, is distressed by her son's question. "They're not teaching anything about Lenin anymore," she told me. "Of course I don't want my kids to worship him, as I was raised to, but I do think they should at least know who he is—it's ridiculous to pretend that Lenin never existed. Lenin is part of who we are, whether we like it or not. But this has always been a country of extremes. With us there are only two possibilities: either slavish idolatry or nothing at all."

Lena was right, I thought. Every nation needs memories—however horrible they might be—because a nation's memories are its roots, and without roots, a nation has no identity. It exists only in the moment.

The Communists tried to persuade everyone that the nation's life began after the Bolshevik Revolution in 1917. Glasnost was an attempt to exhume all the broken pieces of history and put them back together again, but by then so many lies had been told—children's schoolbooks were filled with them—that it was nearly impossible to separate the lies from the truth—to give people their own history back.

Of course the Communists didn't expunge merely the czarist past. They erased parts of their own past too. As the world now knows, even the photographs that appeared in books, newspapers, and magazines were falsified. In one famous photo several of Stalin's political opponents, all of whom had been put to death, were deftly blotted out and replaced by birch trees. Specially trained artists altered the paintings in museums and art galleries, airbrushing Stalin's growing list of enemies from group portraits. Stalin himself, who rarely appeared in public, ordered a painter to do a portrait of him. The five-foot-four dictator wanted to be depicted as tall and imposing, with big, strong hands, and his portrait, which was widely reproduced, shows a towering man with large hands resting majestically on his stomach.

The image of the "Greatest Genius of All Times and Peoples" (as *Pravda* often referred to Stalin) was everywhere—on banners, billboards, even icons—and in the early 1930s Stalin personally oversaw the rewriting of the history of the Soviet Union. Generations of Russians were taught the "Short Course," as it was called, well into the 1980s. Many still don't know that before the revolution, private businesses flourished, a women's movement was bestirring, and trial by jury was de rigueur. In the last instance history had been so thoroughly obliterated that as recently as 1996, I met high-ranking officials in the Justice Ministry who didn't know that after the emancipation of the serfs, Czar Alexander II established a much-admired legal system that included jury trials (they were abolished by the Bolsheviks in 1918).

Soon there will be no one left who is old enough to remember what it was like to live in the Soviet Union. History, this new generation will grow up to believe, began in 1991 with the failed coup against Mikhail Gorbachev. Democracy prevailed, market reforms began, and a country—the Russian Federation—was born.

In the fall of 1995, about a year after I visited the empty graveyard on the embankment, I went to the Museum of the Revolution with Andrei, a friend I saw often. Inside the museum, we put on the special felt slippers visitors are required to wear over their shoes to protect the marble floors.

Shuffling past a large white bust of Lenin, we came to a glass case. Inside was a makeshift room with a small desk, a bed, a television, a lamp, and an old-fashioned radio. I had no idea what the exhibit was supposed to be. But Andrei recognized it immediately as a room in a *kommunalka*, a communal apartment (after the revolution large apartments were nationalized, and several families forced to live together, each confined to one room and sharing the kitchen and bathroom).

"How did you know?" I asked him.

"It looks just like my room at home," he replied grimly. Everything—even the blue-and-white wallpaper—was exactly the same.

I gazed at the communal room inside the glass case. At the bottom, taped to the glass, was a small slip of paper; I hadn't noticed it before. I bent low so that I could read the minute black type: HOUSING IN THE SOVIET PERIOD.

In the *Soviet* period? But millions of people still lived in communal apartments! How, I wondered, were they supposed to react when they saw this?

The display was an absurd lie, and yet here it was: the present masquerading as the past. I suddenly understood why rates of mental illness had risen steadily since the democrats had settled into the Kremlin. The rapid pace of change was simply too much for some people, the experts quoted in newspapers had concluded. But I think there's more to it than that. It was hard enough for people to try to find streets that didn't exist. Now they were being told that they were living in imaginary apartments.

I looked at Andrei. He was still staring at the room. I could tell that he was depressed, but I had the feeling that he would rather not talk about it. Trying to cheer him up, I suggested going to a new café that I had heard about. "You'll like it," I said. "They have espresso and really good *blini*."

We left the museum and took the metro downtown. It took us an hour and a half to find the place. The name of the street had, of course, been changed.

Everyday Calamities in Moscow

BORDER GUARDS SHOULD make sure that everyone entering Russia has a sense of humor. The indignities one must contend with are manifold, and a sense of humor, which is a kind of tonic, is often the only thing that helps. Not long after I arrived in Moscow, I found myself standing in line at the post office to pick up a parcel my mother had sent me. One of the clerks, a stout, jowly woman who looked as though she would feel at home driving a combine on a collective farm, received a telephone call. After listening attentively for some minutes, the clerk, who must have weighed about three hundred pounds and had a tough, pit-bull expression, put her hand on one ample hip and yelled, "And the same to you!" and slammed the phone down hard. She then turned to me and bellowed, "And what do *you* want?"

Such rudeness often takes foreigners by surprise and is particularly disconcerting for Americans, who are accustomed to being served with a smile. Everywhere I went—restaurants, shops, the post office—I saw ill-treated compatriots, the humorless kind who should have been turned away at the border—demanding to see the manager. Confronted with his almost invariable indifference, they usually left, declaring loudly in English that they would never come back to that establishment. My heart went out to them. They did not yet understand that in Russia the customer is always wrong. How different the reaction of most Russians. "*Byvaet*," they say nonchalantly. "It happens."

Russians often mock Americans for our inability to adapt to the difficulties they face every day. Compared with them we Americans *are* helpless. Many of us don't realize just how ill prepared for life we are until we arrive in Russia, where complaining to the manager usually doesn't help and there are no convenient services designed to solve every problem with a toll-free number. In fact, there is no telephone book. As a friend of mine who is a computer buff put it, "Russia isn't user-friendly."

I didn't think that I would be able to buy a shower curtain in Moscow, so I brought one from New York. But when I entered the bathroom of my new apartment, I discovered that there was no shower rod. I had no idea what to do, so I took a shower every morning without a curtain. Since the apartment was so poorly heated that icicles formed along the inside of my bathroom window, this turned into an ordeal. Teeth chattering, I tried to wash as quickly as possible. When I stepped out of the shower, it was so cold that I could feel the ants crawling up and down my spine (as Russians say when they get goose bumps). I donned a superthick robe and walked briskly into my bedroom, prepared to face the elements while getting dressed. The bathroom in my second apartment had no rod either (a common omission, I later learned, since Russians generally take baths, not showers). However, by then I had been living in Moscow for over a year and I was no longer the helpless American. Without a moment's hesitation, I looked around for something I could hang the curtain on and found an old piece of string in one of the kitchen drawers. I then searched all the walls and found two long, sturdy nails. I pulled them out with a hammer, banged one into each side of the bathroom wall, put the string across, and hung up the shower curtain.

By the time my refrigerator broke down in early 1993, I accepted it with a certain Russian stoicism. I took all the food out, opened the door to the balcony, and put it in a soft cushion of snow. I then went back to reading *The Brothers Karamazov*.

"I see that your refrigerator broke down," observed my friend Svetlana as I handed her an orange from the balcony one March afternoon. "When did it happen?"

"Around the middle of January," I replied.

"And you didn't panic?"

"I really didn't give it much thought."

"You mean you just calmly put everything outside? I can't wait to tell my mother this! She'll never believe it. That's just what a Russian would have done—you've become a real Muscovite."

I had no idea what I would do if warmer weather came (the previous spring and summer had been so cold that I had to wear my winter jacket), but I wasn't worried. Having learned how to hang up a shower curtain without a rod, how to do without a refrigerator, and how to fix the toilet when it refused to flush, I had developed a certain confidence, a certain cheek. There was, I felt, no crisis that I couldn't handle.

A winter's night about a year later: I was sitting by the kitchen window, eating kasha and watching the snow fall. The large white flakes were tumbling out of the sky so fast that I could hardly see the street below. There was a knock on the door. "*Minutochku!*" I called out. I peered through the peephole. A pair of large round glasses and a receding hairline came into view. It was Aleksei, my landlord. Standing next to him were a man and two women I had never seen before. I opened the door. One of the women was enormous and had a fleshy black mole the size of a crab apple above her right eye. The other, a *babushka* with a bright floral kerchief tied under her chin, was small and frail looking, with a gray face and long, scraggly hair the same color. The man had a woolly gray beard and a grim, hangdog look. Probably the *babushka*'s husband, I thought. Without a word the women descended on my tiny one-room apartment. The *babushka* peered inside my closets and turned the lights on and off. She then marched into the kitchen and began inspecting the cabinets (I could hear her opening and closing them). Meanwhile Mole Woman waddled into the bathroom and turned on the faucet. The man watched the entire operation from the hallway.

"What's going on here?" I demanded to know.

"Shh! They'll hear you," Aleksei whispered.

"I don't care!" I whispered back. "Who the hell *are* these people?"

"Just pretend that you're my cousin Galya. *Please*. I'll explain later."

Before I could answer, Mole Woman, who was apparently satisfied, turned off the bathroom faucet and waddled back into the room. I was fuming. Aleksei was desperate. And I pretended that my name was Galya.

After they left, Aleksei bowed his head and stared at the floor. When he looked up, his eyes were red and his cheeks were wet with tears. He took off his glasses and sat down on the couch, his gangling frame hunched over. "Olga and I are getting a divorce," he said. His voice was filled with such pain that I felt the tears starting in my own eyes. He and Olga had been married for only two years and had a baby daughter. I didn't know what to say. (Much later I found out that Aleksei, a math professor, couldn't buy Olga the diamonds and designer dresses she craved, and that she had found a rich businessman who could.) "She's selling the apartment to get back at me. You'll have to move out."

"What?" Now I needed to sit down.

"Don't worry, not right away—in a few months. I'm sorry. I know we agreed that you could live here for another year. I wish there were something I could do. You see, the apartment . . . isn't really mine. Well, it belongs to me, but I registered it in Olga's name when we got married. If she wants to sell it, I can't stop her."

I wondered how Aleksei could be so cooperative. Why was he showing prospective buyers the apartment?

And why did I have to pretend that I was his cousin Galya?

"Olga doesn't want people to know that you're a foreigner. It might make them uncomfortable."

Olga was probably right. Many Russians have never traveled beyond the old Iron Curtain simply because they can't afford to do so. As a result of their isolation, such people still view foreigners with suspicion. In their eyes the world is made up of *nashi lyudi*, "our people," and everyone else.

There is the *rodina*, "the motherland," and the rest of the world. To go abroad is to go *za granitsei*, "beyond the frontier." I first became aware of this distinction on the metro, when I sat down next to a beefy Siberian matron who asked if she could borrow my newspaper. I handed her my copy of that day's *Nezavisimaya Gazeta*. After she perused it, we chatted a bit about the latest political crisis. She paused for a moment and studied my face with a puzzled expression. "I can't figure you out," she said. "You look Russian, but you speak with a slight accent. Are you a foreigner or are you one of us?" I told her about my parents and about how I spoke Ukrainian before I spoke English. The woman smiled and said, "Ah, then you are one of us."

(Actually, she told me, there was something besides my accent that had made her wonder whether I might be a foreigner. "You're so skinny," she remarked, looking at me pityingly. "Look at those arms—thin as noodles. And that stomach—where is it? Now *this* is a stomach," she said jovially, patting her own rounded belly with pride. "You need to put on some weight.")

"I'm so sorry about all this," said Aleksei, abruptly bringing my thoughts back to the problem at hand—my imminent eviction. He seemed to be searching for some way to comfort me. But what could he say? "You did a good job, by the way, of pretending, I mean. Thanks for going along with me. You know," he said, touching my hair affectionately, "we *could* pass for cousins. We have the same color hair." I smiled. Such intimate gestures are typical of Russians.

The next day Olga came unannounced. In her tight black leather pants and leopard-print blouse, she looked like a rock star. Her short, spiky black hair, which had a little styling gel in it, added to the effect. Dark eyes flashing, as if ready to take on a challenge, she said, "You have two weeks to find another apartment."

"Two weeks!" I exclaimed. "But Aleksei said that I could stay for a few more months."

"Never mind what Aleksei said. He has no say in this."

"But you know how hard it is to find an apartment in this city."

"All right, I'll give you three weeks, but I *mean* three weeks. When that day comes—I don't care if you've found a new place or not—you have to get out and that's it. Understand?"

I could feel the color drain from my face as panic grabbed me by the throat. How could I have imagined that I was any match for Russia's unpredictable ways?

Looking for an apartment in Moscow is like trying to find an apartment in New York City. Rents downtown are as high as six thousand dollars. Where was I supposed to go?

I had not signed a lease. In Russia no one does; the judicial system is so feeble that written agreements are virtually worthless; verbal agreements are the norm. Since there is no legal recourse should problems arise, people try to judge a prospective landlord's character and preferably rent from someone recommended by a friend.

By the time TASS evicted me (1993), most newspapers had begun to publish apartment listings, but renting from a stranger was risky. I knew people who had found apartments through advertisements, and their landlords threw them out without any notice. The landlords had found someone who could pay more. Being aware of this potential hazard, I had told a close friend that I was looking for an apartment, and she introduced me to Aleksei, whom she had known since high school.

When I first came to take a look at the place, which was on Shosse Entuziastov, the "Highway of the Enthusiasts," I asked Aleksei if I could use the telephone to make sure that it worked reasonably well. "Of course," he said with a smile. "It's right over there." He pointed to a red plastic telephone on a scuffed-up table in the kitchen. I called Tanya, a Canadian friend.

"Can you hear me?" I shouted.

"The line sounds pretty clear," she yelled back. "How's the apartment?"

"Awful, a real hole in the wall, especially the kitchen."

When I put the phone down and saw the look on Aleksei's face, I realized that he had understood everything I had just said.

"You understand English."

"*Da*," he said, no longer smiling.

"I'm sorry, I didn't mean—"

"You Americans are funny, always so apologetic. But tell me, what are you apologizing for? All you did was tell your friend the truth. This apartment is a 'hole in the wall,'" he said, repeating the phrase in English.

We both burst out laughing, and I decided to take the apartment. It was cheap ($160 a month), but, more important, I knew that Aleksei would make a good landlord (I figured that anyone who admitted that his apartment was a hole in the wall couldn't be all bad). He turned out to be ideal. I could always count on him when something needed fixing (except refrigerators), and in the two years that I lived there, he raised the rent only once, by $20, just as he had promised. I would surely miss him. He even offered to help me move. "It's the least I can do," he said. "I don't have a car, but I can help you carry stuff. Call me as soon as you find a place. Here, let me give you my new number."

"You decided to move out?"

"Well, not exactly. Olga threw me out. I'm staying with my mother."

Aleksei took a pen and a piece of paper from my desk, jotted down his mother's number, and handed it to me.

"Thanks," I said, "I'll keep you posted, and don't worry, you'll find a place."

"It's all right. I'm not in any hurry, really. I kind of like living with Mama."

After Olga left that day—slamming the door behind her—I called everyone in my address book, and asked if they knew anyone who was renting an apartment. I wanted to live in the "center," as Russians call the downtown area near the Kremlin, but I couldn't pay more than five hundred dollars a month. (I could have found an apartment in a *spalniy raiyon*, a "sleepy district," relatively easily, but such remote neighborhoods have few, if any, grocery stores and often have little or no public transportation.) Everyone said the same thing: there were no apartments in that location for that price.

So I was surprised when a few people called back with leads. I followed up on all of them, but after two weeks, I still hadn't found anything.

The most frustrating part of my search was that most of the people I called were reluctant to discuss how much they wanted in rent—a vestige of the old Soviet system. Talking about money defiled the socialist ideal. Under Communism, everyone was assigned a job and told what they would be paid. Although the salaries the state doled out were just enough to stave off starvation, people had to pretend that they were satisfied. Why would anyone want more money? Everyone was supposed to be working together to build Communism, and for that, one didn't need money. One could live on enthusiasm. (There is still an enormous billboard on Lusinovskaya Street that says: WE ARE BUILDING COMMUNISM!)

Earning extra money *nye ofitsyalno,* "unofficially"—outside the state enterprise where one worked—was illegal. To take on such work was to expose the inadequacy of the Communist state, which was supposed to provide for its citizens' basic needs, and one had to be punished for that (charities were illegal for the same reason). Money was labeled a "bourgeois concern," something only people in the self-indulgent West talked about.

The harsh realities of market reforms forced people to look for moneymaking opportunities. Many sold their own labor or rented out apartments, preferably for dollars. But a lifetime of conditioning cannot be cast off so easily. Working odd jobs still seemed slightly illicit. Renting out an apartment (state-owned property!) seemed indecent. And so the shamefaced would-be capitalists I encountered skirted the rent issue for as long as they could. How about one of these? they would ask, proffering a box of candy. Would you care for some more tea? When *I* mentioned the word *arenda,* they became flustered and embarrassed. Often they told me that they had no idea how much to charge—it was all so new to them. They needed time to think it over. They would then hurriedly walk me to the elevator, promising to call in a few days.

Most of these people never called. Those who did sounded stiff and uncomfortable, like college kids trying to sell vacuum cleaners over the telephone. When they finally got to the point, they invariably blurted out a price that was way out of my range. One man tried a different tactic: he asked me how much I could afford. When I told him, he sounded incredulous. "That's all?" he said. "No, that won't do."

I did have one asset. I never imagined that being a woman could be an advantage in Russia, but when it comes to apartment hunting, women have a definite edge. Everyone wanted me for a tenant the moment they heard my voice on the telephone and many people invited me to come see their apartment immediately. Renting to a man was *isklucheno*—out of the question—they told me. One woman clutched her head with both hands as she recalled what happened when she rented out her one-bedroom apartment to a seemingly respectable financier. "Oh, the loud parties he would throw. They lasted until morning, some of them. Once, when I came upstairs, I found empty beer bottles all over the place and two women sleeping on the floor. One of them was practically naked! Can you imagine? I should have known better. That's the way it is with men. They'll turn the place into a brothel. It's much better to rent to a nice, quiet young lady," she said, patting my hand. This is it, I thought. I can stop looking. But after three cups of tea and two pieces of apple crumb cake, I discovered that she wanted "a nice, quiet young lady" who could pay nine hundred dollars a month.

I had just five days left. I was so tense that I could hardly sleep. One night I dreamed that a bunch of men in black ski masks stormed my apartment and dragged me out. When I asked them who their commander was, they pointed to a doorway, where Olga suddenly materialized, dressed in a sleek purple catsuit with matching wraparound sunglasses. I pleaded with her, but she merely sneered and whipped out an official-looking document. When I looked closely, I saw that it was a warrant for my arrest.

Three days before my deadline, a breakthrough: I remembered that there was one person in my address book whom I hadn't been able to reach. Heidi, an American, was a freelance photographer, which meant that, like me, she probably didn't have much money, so her rent had to be low. I had run into her once in front of Pizza Hut, which was in the "center," and she had said that she lived nearby. Maybe, I thought, as I dialed her number, she knew of other inexpensive apartments in the area. It turned out that Heidi was moving out that very week and that her landlord had asked her if she knew anyone—preferably a woman—who was looking for an apartment. Would I like to see the place? The rent was $530, but Yura, the landlord, was planning to raise it, by how much she didn't know. I called Yura and asked him. "We'll talk about that when you get here," he replied.

I took the trolleybus downtown and met Yura in the lobby. As we climbed a narrow staircase, he told me that the building was built in the 1930s and that the apartment had belonged to one of Stalin's generals. At that time it was a grand affair, eight enormous rooms. But the general fell victim to one of Stalin's political purges. After he was shot, the apartment was confiscated, and each room was converted into a self-contained apartment, complete with kitchen and bathroom. Suddenly one apartment metamorphosed into eight apartments. "That was one of the ways that our wondrous state dealt with the housing shortage," Yura said dryly. "They killed off someone important and then carved up the apartment." All the photographs the general left behind were burned. Everything else was carted away: all the expensive furniture and fine china, all the antique silverware, even his wife's jewelry.

"What happened to the wife?" I asked.

"She was declared an 'enemy of the people' and sent to a labor camp. I believe she died there."

When we got to the third floor, Yura took out a big silver key and opened a wooden door that had been painted dark brown. We entered a large, dimly lit corridor. There were four steel doors on each side, all covered with the same brown leather padding. Taking out another, smaller key, Yura opened the second door on the left. There was a small entrance hall and then a room with an alcove. The room wasn't very large, but I was used to living in cramped quarters (Aleksei's apartment was so small that I had to move the washing machine every time I wanted to get into the kitchen). Connected to the entrance hall were a miniature bathroom and a kitchen, also of Lilliputian proportions. A colorful tapestry hanging next to the refrigerator caught my eye. It was an intricately embroidered picture of a *babushka* drawing a bucket of water from a well. What caught my attention was the way the tapestry was positioned—it was crooked, as though someone had hung it there in a hurry. When I lifted it, I discovered what looked like a trapdoor. It was about the size of a mini-refrigerator and had been painted shut.

"What is *this*?" I asked Yura.

"That used to be a secret passageway. It led to an underground tunnel. This way the general could make a quick escape if he needed to. Our leaders were quite paranoid; they were always afraid that someone might try to assassinate them. I guess it never occurred to him that the people he trusted the most would get him in the end."

"What's that?" I asked, pointing to a small device on the ceiling that looked like an intercom.

"A very sophisticated smoke alarm. It had a special cooling system that would keep the temperature inside the apartment from getting too hot so that the general and his wife would have more time to get out."

"Does it still work?"

"I doubt it."

"Are there any other curiosities?"

"That's about it. So, are you interested?"

"How much is the rent?"

I expected Yura to break out the samovar. But he looked me right in the eye and said, "Five hundred and seventy dollars."

It was relatively cheap, but still more than I could comfortably afford.

In Russia haggling is part of everyday life. One haggles with vendors in outdoor markets, cabdrivers, even customs officials. Why not try it with a landlord?

"The rent is a bit expensive for me," I ventured. "Would you be willing to accept five hundred?"

Yura thought for a moment. A man who came earlier in the week had offered him six hundred. "Let's make it five fifty."

"How about five twenty?"

"All right, five twenty it is. Better to rent the apartment for less money to someone reliable than to rent it out to some rich businessman who'll probably destroy the place. Then what good will all that money do me? I'll have to spend half of it on repairs."

"Thank you," I said, smiling.

That's when I noticed the cockroach. It was about two inches long and it was crawling on a wall in the kitchen. Yura took off his shoe and hit it. It fell to the floor. Its body was crushed, but its legs were still moving, so Yura stepped on it. The legs stopped moving. Slipping back into his shoe, he turned to me and said, "So, when would you like to move in?"

As I stared at the big brown stain the cockroach had left on the flowery wallpaper, I recalled something that happened at TASS. One evening I was talking on the telephone when something fell from the ceiling and landed on my head: tiny legs were crawling across my scalp. I dropped the receiver and slapped my head vigorously, trying to get the loathsome creature out of my hair. I would have let out a scream, but there were a dozen other people in the office, quietly going about their work. (I was sitting all the way in the back, so they couldn't see what was going on.) Bending over, I tore at my hair; the cockroach finally fell out. I looked at the floor. Where did it go? There it was, scurrying under the desk.

Quickly I moved the chair I had been sitting on and stepped on the cockroach with my big fur boot, crushing it. I then returned to my seat and picked up the receiver. "Sorry about that," I said to the editor on the other end. "I had to take care of something."

Not wanting to go through *that* again, I asked Yura if he would hire an exterminator before I moved in. He seemed to think me squeamish.

"But there are roaches everywhere," he said. "Don't you have them in your USA?"

"Well, yes, but—"

"All right, if it's that important to you. I'll call someone tomorrow."

My next task was to figure out how to move all my belongings. The last time I moved (to Aleksei's apartment), I had enlisted the services of a state-run moving company. I had told the man who answered the telephone that I would need a large truck and two movers. He said that I should come to his office the day of my move and he would take care of everything. But when I arrived he was nowhere to be found, and no one there seemed to know what I was talking about. "Excuse me," I said to a middle-aged woman with a red peasant scarf tied around her head. The woman, who was sitting on a chair in a corner, reading the newspaper, didn't look up. "*Devushka*," I said, in an attempt to get her attention. Now that the word "comrade" has been jettisoned along with the Soviet Union, people have no idea what to call one another. Curiously, it is socially acceptable to address a man simply as *muzhshina* (man), as in "Excuse me, man, can you tell me where the post office is?" But addressing a woman as *zhenshina* (woman) is considered rude because it implies that she is no longer young. The preferred term is *devushka* (girl), regardless of the woman's age. (I have seen sixty-year-old heads turn at the sound of the word, particularly in shops. Since one is not allowed to touch the merchandise, and getting served depends entirely on the goodwill of the surly matrons who work as salesclerks, everyone always addresses them as "*devushka*.")

The woman put down her newspaper and glowered at me. "What's your problem?"

"I need a couple of movers. I was told to come in today, but—"

"Can't you see that I'm busy?"

I remembered something a Russian acquaintance told me: "One must always solve all problems in the morning. In the afternoons no one answers the telephone, and no one feels like working."

One must always solve all problems in the morning. Of course. What had I been thinking? It was already 12:30 in the afternoon. (So tired was I after spending most of the night packing that I had hit the snooze button on my alarm clock and overslept.) But the housing department at TASS had told me that my successor was coming (from England) that very evening, and they had already promised him my apartment.

I left the office and hurried into the courtyard, where I could see a group of burly men in grimy blue jackets, smoking and drinking next to a few large trucks. "Hey, why don't you have some vodka with us?" one of them jeered, flashing two stubby yellow teeth. I ignored him and explained my plight to the man sitting next to him, whose unshaven face had a serious expression. He was tall and red-haired and had a potbelly, though he was probably still in his early thirties. His sleeves were rolled up; on his right arm was a tattoo of an elephant and a showgirl.

"It won't take long," I said, "maybe an hour or so. I'll pay you well."

"The boss isn't here," he told me.

"I know. I had an appointment with him."

"I can't do anything until the boss gets here."

"Do you know when he'll be in?"

"How should I know?"

He took a deck of cards out of his pocket and turned to his colleagues. "Hey, guys, wanna play?"

Finally two movers agreed to help me, but one of them kept calling me *moya lapochka*, "my little paw," a term of endearment in Russian, and the other was so drunk that he could hardly walk, much less carry anything.

I dreaded having to deal with such ineptitude again, but there didn't seem to be any alternative. That moving company was the only one in Moscow (the state had a monopoly on just about every kind of service). Then I asked myself: What would a Russian do in this situation? I put on my coat and went outside. Standing on the curb, I flagged down a bus. "Listen," I said to the driver, "I'm moving tomorrow morning. I'll pay you fifty dollars if you help me."

"Where are you moving to?"

"Bolshaya Dorogomilovskaya Street. Do you know where that is?"

"Sure."

"Can you meet me here at eight o'clock sharp with the bus?"

"No problem."

He closed the doors.

"Wait!" I motioned to him to reopen the doors. "What's your name?"

"Valentin Vasilyevich." And he shut the doors and drove off.

True to his word, Valentin showed up promptly at eight the next morning—completely sober. He was quite courteous and even helped Aleksei and me carry my washing machine into the bus. By the time we were finished, all the seats were taken up by my belongings and there was just enough room for Aleksei and me to sit down.

Valentin revved up the engine, and the bus rumbled into the early morning traffic. Cars were honking, and a milk truck suddenly swerved in front of us. Valentin's face turned red as he maneuvered the bus out of the way.

"Isn't this the bus that goes to October Square?" I asked him, naming a major route.

"Yes, it is."

"What did you tell your boss, if you don't mind me asking?"

He looked perplexed. "I didn't tell him anything. If he asks me what happened, I'll just say that I got a flat tire. But I doubt that he'll find out. No one will say anything about the bus not coming. It's normal."

A Little Help from My "Russian Mother"

THE SOVIET STATE HAD a voracious appetite for the intimate details of its subjects' lives. It eavesdropped on telephone conversations, intercepted packages, and read letters. Of course people were watched, at work (everyone knew that the "personnel department" was just another arm of the KGB) and at school. Libraries, doctor's offices, and churches were hotbeds of surveillance, too.

There was only one place where one could escape from the prying eyes of the state: an apartment. Perhaps this is why Russians have always been so devoted to their homes, infusing them with *uyutnost*, the kind of love and care that makes even the shabbiest apartment look warm and inviting. As Lena said when I complimented her on the ingenuity with which she had decorated her small two-room walk-up, "You may not be able to talk freely on the telephone or even much at all if your ceiling is bugged—in that case you have to write notes or use hand signals—but at least the state can't *see* you." (In the mid-1990s wiretapping and bugging were still legal.)

It wasn't long before I, too, began to view my apartment as my only refuge. It was the spring of 1993, and I was on my way home from a birthday party. I boarded a bus, transferred twice, then took a tram—and so did two men in dark suits. Maybe they were going in the same direction, I thought. Maybe they weren't what they looked like. But after I got off the tram, they introduced themselves and showed me their internal passports, which clearly identified them with one of the most feared organizations in the world. I opened each man's little red booklet, which bore the gold hammer and sickle on the cover. There it was in bold print: *Kommitet Gosudarstvennoi Bezopasnosti*, the Committee for State Security.

"Documents!" commanded one of the agents, a tall, square-jawed man with a blond buzz cut.

I took out my passport and handed it to him.

"Do you know who we are?" he asked as he studied my picture.

"You're with the KGB."

"*Molodetz*. Smart girl. Not all Americans know our full name. They expect to see the letters *KGB*, like in the movies."

The other agent, who was short and powerfully built, like a prizefighter, laughed contemptuously.

Oddly enough, they asked for my telephone number. I took out a slip of paper and wrote it down. They seemed satisfied, and I thought that they would let me go, but then Pint-Size Boxer said that they would accompany me to my door.

"It's for your own safety," he told me. "We're protecting you."

"From whom?"

"Anyone who may wish to harm you."

"Thank you, but that really isn't necessary."

"Ah, but it is," said Square Jaw.

As we walked to my apartment, which was about three blocks away, our conversation centered on the usual topics that strangers might talk about: the high price of food, how many children they had, where they would be vacationing that summer. But their presence was unnerving, especially when they called me *grazhdanka*, citizen. "Citizen" is what prisoners are called in jail. It is also the form of address used by police or KGB when they are about to make an arrest. I kept asking myself the same question: what could they possibly want with a small-fry journalist like me? When we finally reached my door, the two men told me to enjoy my stay in Moscow and left. (I never saw or heard from them again.)

Weeks later I was still spooked. How long had they been watching me?

I would never know.

Closing my door at the end of the day, I would often think: at least no one can spy on me in here.

So, when I moved into my new apartment, dingy as it was, I was determined to turn it into a home. But how do you do that in a country where you have to stand in three different lines to buy anything, and half the things you need aren't available anyway?

Decorating the apartment would have presented a challenge even in the best of circumstances. The bathroom was a kaleidoscope of colors. The sink was green; the bathtub was blue; and the tiles were purple, yellow, and pink. In the room were long, dark brown curtains with tiny red crabs and seashells along the border. And then there was the couch, which was neon orange with shaggy black stripes that resembled those on a tiger's coat. It was the first thing I saw when I opened my eyes in the morning and it never failed to depress me. To make matters worse, all the windows were enclosed by a sort of concrete awning, so that no sunlight could come in, which made the apartment dark and dreary even in the morning.

I tried everything I could think of to brighten it up. I scrubbed the place clean, polishing the grimy floors and cupboards until they shone. I bought pretty little baskets of artificial flowers, lace doilies, and all sorts of other bibelots. I even splurged on a beautiful antique-style coffee table (the one that upset the TV repairman and enchanted Lyudmila). That purchase required a bit more effort than the others. As I stood on the curb outside the furniture shop, struggling to balance the heavy table with one hand while trying to hail a cab with the other, a truck drove through a large puddle. I moved out of the way to avoid getting splashed, slipped on a patch of ice, and nearly fell into a snowbank. At last a car stopped and the driver rolled down the window.

"Can you take me to Bolshaya Dorogomilovskaya Street?"

"How much?" he asked gruffly.

"Twenty thousand rubles," I answered. That was a lot of money for such a short ride, the equivalent of four dollars to go two blocks, but I was desperate.

"*Nyet.*"

"Why not?"

"I would have to make a U-turn," he said wearily. To do so legally would mean driving several kilometers. It was really just too much trouble.

"This table is heavy. I don't think I can carry it the rest of the way. I'll pay you seventy thousand rubles [ten dollars]."

"I don't have time," he said and sped off.

I tried two more drivers, but the response was the same, and in the end I had to walk. My arms were throbbing with pain, and I had to put the table down every few minutes so that I could rest; what should have been a fifteen-minute walk stretched into forty-five minutes. When I finally made it back to my apartment, I positioned the table directly in front of the couch.

Then I set out to find artificial roses. I looked every-where, but the dime-store plastic variety were all that was available. After a week I was just about ready to give up. Then one cold and rainy morning, as I was riding the escala-tor into the dank, cavernous metro, I spotted a woman in a black fur hat selling dainty pink roses made of silk, with little clusters of baby's breath surrounding a few of the closed buds. I bought two small bunches and put them in a crystal vase, which I placed on the coffee table.

I had hoped that the table and the roses would draw attention away from the couch. But no matter what I did, the couch was the first thing that everyone noticed.

"So what do you think of the place?" I asked Svetlana, who came over one morning to go shopping with me for a tablecloth (to cover up the fist-size hole in the middle of the kitchen table).

"What a vile couch." She reached out and touched one of its tiger stripes. "My God, it looks like it's alive."

Something had to be done. I thought maybe I could have the couch reupholstered, but I had no idea how to find a good upholsterer (or any upholsterer) in Moscow. None of my Russian friends could think of a single place that did such work. When there was still a Soviet Union, Svetlana said dolefully, there were lots of upholstery shops, but all the ones she knew of had been bought by private companies and transformed into casinos, fast-food restaurants, or X-rated video salons. She advised me to try a few state-run furniture shops: "If you offer them enough money, they might agree to do it."

At the first three shops, the person who answered the telephone simply said, "*Nyet*" and hung up. The woman who picked up the phone at the fourth shop said they didn't upholster couches, they only sold furniture. Following Svetlana's advice, I said that I would be willing to pay her "*mnogo deneg* [a lot of money]." She asked me where I lived. When I told her, she said, "*Devushka*, that's too far. I would have to take the trolleybus. It would take me at least ten minutes to get there. I don't think so." And then she, too, hung up.

The next day I went to a novelty shop in my neighborhood to buy a lamp. A few chunky *babushki* were standing in front of the shop, holding handmade sweaters, shawls, hats, and mittens between frozen fingers, hoping that someone might buy them. I came there so often that a few of the *babushki* recognized me and waved. "*Zdrastvuytye!* Hello!" shouted one, flashing a wide smile with a few brilliant silver teeth. "Nice to see you!" I yelled back. I noticed a few new faces. Among them was a rough-hewn woman holding the most exquisite shawl I had ever seen. It was white and had an intricate gold filigree design. She was obviously a talented craftswoman—I suddenly had an idea: maybe *she* could reupholster my couch.

From a distance the woman looked as hard and sturdy as a tank, but as I drew closer, I saw that her face was soft and round and that she had the pink cheeks of a child. I introduced myself. Looking like she didn't know quite what to make of me, but figuring, I suppose, that I looked harmless enough, the woman told me that her name was Nina Mikhailovna Trudolyubova (which means "one who loves work"). "Lori," she repeated. "That's not a Russian name. You must be a foreigner. Where are you from?" When I told her, her blue eyes widened. "America? Well, God help you, what are you doing in a country like this? Don't you miss your parents?"

I had been asked this question many times. Russians, who often have extremely close relationships with their parents, cannot understand the American tug toward independence, our willingness to move hundreds, even thousands of miles from our parents. I said that I was used to living on my own. A look of pain came into Nina's eyes when I mentioned that I had moved out at twenty-three, and that my parents initially felt hurt by my decision, but eventually accepted it as an inevitable consequence of my Americanization. "Your poor mother. She must have been heartbroken. Does she have any other children?"

"I have an older sister and a younger brother."

"And have they abandoned her too?"

"My sister lives in Connecticut—that's one of our states. She moved out when she got married eleven years ago."

"Well, that's understandable. And your brother?"

"He lives at home."

"There's a good boy. And what about your motherland? You must miss it."

"I do miss New York sometimes, but right now I have a bigger problem."

I explained that I had just settled into a new apartment and that I was stuck with a couch that I couldn't bear to look at—I desperately wanted to cover it up somehow, to have it reupholstered perhaps, but I couldn't find anyone to do it. When I described what the couch looked like, Nina's plump hands flew to her cheeks.

"Orange and black? Oh, how awful that must look! You unfortunate girl!"

Her eyes were filled with sympathy. But then she said, "I can't help you. I can make things like this [she held up the shawl], but I don't know anything about reupholstering couches. I just don't think I'm the right person to do it. You need a pair of strong arms. How would I turn the couch over? That's a man's job." Besides, where in heaven's name were we going to find the right kind of material? There used to be some lovely *kamka* (damask) in a state store over on Leninski Prospekt, but she hadn't been there since Brezhnev was in power, and God only knew what they were selling now, probably imported cars. And Nina Mikhailovna Trudolyubova rolled her eyes in disgust at the thought of all those imported cars that only a handful of people—all those rich ex-Communists who had gone into business—could afford to buy.

I said that I already had some material that I thought would do nicely. Nina stared at me. I wondered what she was thinking, but I couldn't tell from her expression. Afraid that I would be stuck with the neon-tiger couch forever, I told her that I had tried everything and that I had nowhere else to turn. I explained how dreary my apartment looked and how much I wanted to turn it into a home. She continued to regard me silently. I was beginning to feel awkward. This was a crazy idea. Why should she help me? I was a complete stranger.

Just as I was about to apologize and walk away, Nina smiled, revealing a gold front tooth. "I like you," she declared. "I so respect young people who try to make their homes look cozy. It's a rare thing nowadays. My son and daughter-in-law could have such a lovely apartment if only they would put a little time and effort into fixing it up, but they're part of this new, on-the-go generation—busy making money. Every time I come over—you can imagine what it looks like when I'm not there—there are dishes in the sink, and there's dust all over the place. They've been married for ten years, and their apartment still doesn't look like a home. Some people just don't have the touch, I guess."

"My apartment's not far from here," I ventured. "If you don't mind—if you're not too busy—maybe we could go there now and you could have a look at my couch?"

"Well, all right, but I'm just going to take a look at it, mind you. I'm not making any promises."

When we got to my apartment, I took out the two large *pokrivali* (thick pieces of material) I had bought in a rich ochre with undertones of bronze and copper. Nina draped one *pokrivala* over the couch, and took a step back, the way that an artist moves away from her easel. Wrinkling her forehead, she studied the couch, surveying it from various angles. Yes, she pronounced at last, there was hope. She would come back next week with her sewing box, and she would see what she could do. "But remember, I've never done this before, so don't expect miracles." There was one glitch, she said, as she put on her worn leather boots: she lived in Podolsk, which was two hours from Moscow by *elektrichka*, the local train. It was a long way to travel, and she would need to make several trips. I suggested that she bring her nightgown and stay at my apartment. (I felt, intuitively, that I could trust her, and she seemed to feel the same way about me—she accepted my invitation unreservedly.)

Nina came back the following Tuesday, but she didn't bring her nightgown and she wouldn't hear of going to sleep. At ten o'clock that night, her plump figure was still bent over the couch. She was so absorbed in her task that she didn't hear me come in from the kitchen. She had cut some material and was fastening it to the couch with a few pins, which she withdrew from a little white basket that was on the floor. She looked up for a moment and smiled. "You go to sleep, dear. Don't let me disturb you."

At around 10:30, I finally persuaded her to sit down and have some hot chocolate with me. I had the Russian kind, which is as rich and thick as a milkshake. Made by the Lenin Factory, it came in a little yellow box that had a picture of Lenin on it. I heated some milk, stirred in a few spoonfuls of the cocoa, along with a dash of sugar, and poured the mixture into two teacups. As we sat at my kitchen table, sipping the warm, comforting *kakao*, Nina told me all about her life, about how she had knitted socks and sewed clothes for her children during the war while her husband was at the front; how she sold her grandmother's jewelry and did odd jobs, like chopping wood, to keep the family from starving. Even so they lived mostly on bread, which she baked herself with flour that she hoarded away in her cupboard before the war. She told me about her husband, who never

e our little project. Sometimes she would look around
apartment and smile to herself, as if she were thinking, I
't believe I did all this.

She always came with a small plastic bag. Pulling out
hatever she had made, she would say, "If you don't like it,
st tell me. I'll take it for myself and make you another
he."

Whenever I asked Nina how much I should pay her, she
verted her gaze and said softly, "Whatever you decide will
be fine." And that was all she would say. Like the prospective landlords I met after Olga evicted me, Nina, who had
grown up under Stalin, still felt uncomfortable accepting
money that did not come from the state. So I would wait
until one of those occasional nights when she would stay
over and take a bath, and then I would slip some money
into her coat pocket.

One day she took two handmade doilies out of her little
bag. One was white. The other was the color of coffee with
milk.

"I hope you like them," she said.

"I do, very much."

"Oh, I'm so glad! I put my heart into every stitch, and it
makes me happy when the things I create bring joy into
people's lives."

"There's just one thing. I didn't—"

"I know, I know, you didn't ask me to make them, but I
wanted to. Think of me as your Russian mother," she said,
pinching my cheek. She told me that she had always wanted
a daughter, and that I was just about the right age and, it
was obvious, in need of a mother. How, she wondered, could

made it back—she found out about his death by telegram—
and about her other son, who, at forty, still lived with her
and was an alcoholic.

"I try to keep the bottle away from him, but it's no use.
He's just like his father. I tell him, 'You drink because your
heart is full of pain, but you can't spend your life drinking
and feeling sorry for yourself. Do you think that I have no
pain? Of course I do, but you don't see me drinking my life
away.' I have known very little joy. . . ."

She took out a handkerchief and wiped the tears from
her eyes.

I clasped her hand.

"I'm all right," she said, squeezing my hand and smiling
through her tears.

She soon recovered her good humor and sent me to bed
with gentle admonishments ("Come on now, it's getting late.
Look, it's past midnight already") while she herself went
back to work. I lay in bed in the little alcove, which was just
a few feet away from the couch. I tried to stay awake to
keep Nina company, but eventually drifted off into a deep
sleep.

When I woke up the next morning, I could hardly believe my eyes. The couch, once so hideous, was beautiful. It
was as though a winged fairy had come during the night
and touched it with her magic wand.

"What do you think?" Nina asked, smiling.

"It's lovely," I said, hugging her. The entire room suddenly looked brighter.

I noticed that Nina was pale. She looked tired.

"Ninochka," I said, "you didn't stay up all night, did
you?"

"Actually I did."

"But you must be exhausted. Why don't you lie down on the couch—or better yet, on my bed—and I'll make you some breakfast. What would you like? Scrambled eggs? Or kasha maybe?"

"No, no, don't trouble yourself. I'm not hungry—honestly—and I'm not that tired. I'm a *sova*, a night owl. I like staying up late." She checked her watch. "Oh, my, I've got to go. I have to catch the *elektrichka*. I wish that I could stay here for a while, like we planned, but my son needs me."

Nina put on her coat and hat and hurried out the door. From the kitchen window I could see her nimble figure crossing the courtyard. She looked up and when she saw me, she smiled, her gold tooth gleaming in the morning sun. I smiled back and watched her cantaloupe-colored hat until it rounded the corner and disappeared.

Now all I needed were matching pillows and curtains. During the next few weeks I learned the Russian words for "ruffle," "organza," and "lace." On a couple of occasions I forgot one of these key words, and Nina and I both laughed at my feeble attempts to explain what I meant. I made a few sketches, but they were rather crude, and I was afraid that she might not understand what I wanted. But she always came back with an even more perfect version of whatever I had envisioned. She made two sets of curtains: short, sungold ones for the window behind the couch, and another, floor-length set, which I planned to hang in front of the alcove to create the illusion of another room. These were a shimmering white and were as delicate as moonlight. She

also made three champagne-colored sa[...] with white lace, for the couch.

Next on the agenda: the kitchen. Ni[...] border to the plain white tablecloth I l[...] matching red slipcovers with white ruffles [...] artificial flower arrangement with lots of [...] embroidered picture of a mouse in a chef's [...] red apron added the finishing touch, giving the[...] ful, festive look, like one of those kitchens in t[...] issue of a women's magazine.

Of course the world outside my door was[...] Old tires, rusty auto parts, and broken beer bott[...] my street, and the endless rows of run-down apartm[...] ings were only slightly obscured by the unremitt[...] ness of the sky.

But I took such pleasure in the transformation [...] apartment that I hardly noticed the dismal landscape[...] whenever I went out, I actually found myself lookin[...] ward to coming home. Walking briskly from the met[...] my apartment, I eyed the hillocks of ripe tomatoes that w[...] sold on street corners along the way and suddenly notic[...] how round and red and delicious they looked. Often, i[...] stopped to buy a kilo, I would chat with the vendor as [...] removed one black glove and reached into my handbag to[...] pull out a few thousand rubles. The vendor, usually a hefty woman with a permanent scowl, always looked a little startled by my overture but frequently responded with a smile and a "*Vsevo Khoroshevo!* All the best to you!"

As my spirits soared, so did Nina's. Her face was animated and her voice exuberant whenever she came to conmy own mother have let me go abroad—and to a *dikaya strana*, "wild country" like Russia, no less—all by myself, at the tender age of twenty-five. Whenever I saw Nina in her floppy hat, a few tendrils of her curly white hair sticking out a little, I wanted to pinch her cheek, too.

Once, just before she dashed off, she presented me with a golden box tied with a red satin ribbon.

"This is for your mother," she said. "I don't know her, but I'm sure that she's a good woman. She does like chocolate, I hope?"

"She loves chocolate. Ninochka, I'm touched. But these look awfully expensive."

She waved her hand dismissively. "Not at all. They came in a plain brown box. I put them into this one and added the ribbon myself."

"*Spasibo bolshoye*, from my mother and from me." I kissed Nina on both cheeks, and she enveloped me in a bear hug.

* * *

Nina culled the material for almost everything she made from an enormous black trunk filled with the kinds of things that only a Russian would save: the linings from the insides of old winter coats (which she used to make the pillows for the couch and the ribbon for the box of chocolates), lace from old-fashioned handkerchiefs (the trimming for the pillows and the embroidered mouse's apron), and even tattered socks and panty hose with runs (stuffing for the pillows and filler material for the floral arrangement).

The only thing she insisted on was that I buy my own material for the curtains. This proved to be a challenge, since I had to figure out how much material I needed without a ruler, one of the many trivial items that no shop seemed to carry. Looking around my apartment for a suitable substitute, my eyes zeroed in on my desk: there, next to my laptop, was a narrow strip of plastic with an explanation of all the keys. It was just the right size—about an inch wide and roughly twelve inches long.

I took the metro to a privately owned shop, where I had spotted the perfect fabric. When the salesclerk asked me how many meters I wanted, I whipped out my makeshift ruler and said, "I'm sorry, but I don't have a ruler. I used this instead and came up with 8 ¹/₂." She didn't look at all surprised. Without a word she took the piece of plastic from my hand and measured out the fabric.

The transformation took about three months. By the time Nina and I were finished, she had earned $250 (about fifteen times her monthly pension), and I had an apartment that looked as snug as any in Russia.

"How in the world did you manage all this?" asked Lena, who saw the apartment when I first moved in. "It looks like something out of a fable." Rita, another friend, pronounced me a *nastoyashchaya khozyaika*, "a real homemaker"—the highest accolade one can bestow on a woman in Russia. "Now all you need is a husband," she said with a wink. Even Yura, my crusty landlord, smiled approvingly. "It's so cozy," he said, sitting down on my newly upholstered couch and looking around the room. "If I didn't know better, I would think that I had walked into the wrong apartment."

The only one who hadn't seen my newly decorated apartment yet was Svetlana. She had promised to come at six o'clock, and it was almost seven. Where could she be? I was about to call her when the doorbell—actually a recording of birds chirping—rang. A few seconds later I heard another flutter of birds. That had to be Svetlana, she always rang twice. I undid the chain lock and opened the door. She was holding a plate covered with a plastic shopping bag. (In Russia there is no such thing as aluminum foil or plastic wrap.)

"Sorry I'm late," she said. "The trolleybus broke down, and I had to wait for another one. Look what I baked: a blueberry *perok*." She knew that Russian pastry was my favorite. "It smells wonderful," I said, taking the plate from her.

Fine-boned and slender, with a strikingly white complexion and Tatar eyes, Svetlana reminded me of a princess I once saw in a children's storybook. Looking stylish in a long black skirt and a silky orange blouse, she stood in front of the full-length mirror in the entrance hall and ran a comb through her shiny black hair. Having completed this ritual, which she always performed immediately after arriving, she tucked the comb back into her handbag and followed me into the kitchen.

"Let me help you," she said, rolling up her sleeves and reaching into one of the drawers for a knife.

"I'm just about done," I said, chopping up a potato and adding it to the *svekolnik* (beet soup) I was making.

Svetlana picked up a wooden spoon that was lying on the counter and tasted the soup.

"How is it?" I asked.

She made a face. "Too bland. Actually it tastes terrible—but it's not as bad as it was the last time."

(I was stunned and hurt by such remarks when I first moved to Moscow, but I soon realized that Russians simply did not believe in false praise.)

I took the spoon from Svetlana and tasted the soup myself. She was right. It *was* bland.

"I'm just going to add some more salt and pepper," I told her. "Sit down on the couch and relax. I'll be there in a minute." Like every Russian woman I know, Svetlana is a fantastic cook, and I could have used her help in the kitchen, but I was trying to maneuver her into the room. I was curious what she would say when she saw the couch.

A few minutes later I brought in the pot of *svekolnik* and set it down on the coffee table, along with two plates and two spoons.

"What's the matter?" I asked. "You look upset."

"I am. My secretary made a mess of the report I asked her to type this morning. There was no time to redo it and I had to send it to the Justice Ministry like that. They're going to wonder what kind of lawyer could possibly submit such garbage.

"I should have known better," Svetlana added. "A woman is a fool by nature."

"Svetlana, how can you say such a thing? *You're* a woman!"

"Yes, I know, don't remind me," she said brusquely. "But I had no choice in the matter. Anyway, I'm not typical. From the time I was a schoolgirl, I knew that I was different from the others. They were all so silly. I was much more independent, more logical. . . ."

As Svetlana talked I thought of a passage from "Mire," one of Chekhov's short stories: "A woman . . ." says the Jewess disdainfully. "It's not my fault that God has cast me into this mould, is it? The violin is not responsible for the choice of its case. I am very fond of myself, but when anyone reminds me that I am a woman, I begin to hate myself. . . ." Before I met Svetlana, I thought that such women existed only in Chekhov's imagination.

Svetlana took a drag of her cigarette and blew the smoke out of the corner of her mouth. Crossing her black-stockinged legs, she continued haughtily, "I thought less about my future as a wife and mother [than the other girls] and more about what I was going to *do* with my life. Some of those girls did manage to reach a high level of achievement in science or politics or whatever, but they put their energies into their careers for the sole reason that no one chose them—they had no one to cook cabbage soup for. I pursued a career not from sheer boredom or loneliness, but because it was something I really wanted."

She went on to discuss her secretary's many faults—and those of women in general.

"Most women can't be trusted with a secret. They're such Judases! You're better off confiding in a man."

Silently I reminded myself of Svetlana's good points. She was fond of animals; watching her with Engelbert, her gray tabby, I saw her gentle side. It came out at other times too. Whenever I had a cold, she brought me oranges and medicinal herbs. Once she even came with a thermometer and insisted on taking my temperature.

I think she was greatly influenced by her chauvinistic father. He was a *voyeniy*, a military man, and although he had long since retired, his uniform, which was plumed with medals, still hung on the door of his bedroom closet. Freshly ironed and ramrod straight, with a pair of polished black boots directly underneath the trousers, it looked as though it might salute you and march across the room. I once overheard him tell his wife that she had no sense. "Long in hair, short in brains," he added, repeating a popular Russian folk saying. "A chicken is not a bird; a woman is not a person," was another proverb I heard him fling at Svetlana's mother.

Whenever Svetlana lambasted women, I tried to remember her upbringing. Usually I merely listened to her harangues. I knew that if I said anything in defense of our sex, she would say that I was talking like a *feministka* and we would only get into an argument. That evening I waited until I couldn't stand it any longer. Then I changed the subject.

"You haven't told me what you think of the apartment."

"Well, this new couch is definitely an improvement. How did you persuade your landlord to let you get rid of that beastly one?"

"I didn't persuade him."

"What? You mean this is the same couch?"

She got up and ran her fingers along one of the arms. "Not bad," she said admiringly. "I gather that this is the *babushka*'s handiwork? Well, the old lady obviously knows what she's doing. You can't even see the stitches—it looks as though a professional upholsterer did it. It changes the whole look of the place."

She surveyed the room. As she walked past the alcove, the long, gossamer curtains billowed out. "These are absolutely gorgeous," she said, touching the curtains. "Now the apartment looks fit for human beings."

I owed Nina so much. Somehow, the money I paid her didn't seem to be enough. I wanted to do something special for her. So, one night when we were chatting on the telephone, I asked her whether she had ever thought about going into business.

"Me? Go into business? But *milaya*, dear one, I don't know anything about such things."

I finally persuaded her to let me place an advertisement in the *Moscow Times*, an English-language newspaper. Nina scolded me for "wasting money" on her, but giggled with delight when I translated the text I had come up with. The advertisement, which ran for four weeks, read:

Want to turn your grim apartment into a home? Call Babushka, Inc. I custom-make curtains, pillows, tablecloths, doilies, bedspreads, chair covers, slipcovers, and whatever else you need to make your apartment look bright and cheerful. All prices negotiable. Call Nina Mikhailovna Trudolyubova: 531–9640. Speak Russian.

A few weeks later my telephone rang. It was Nina. She sounded excited, but there was so much static on the line that I could hardly make out what she was saying. When the crackling finally stopped, I heard her say that a few people had called from Moscow and asked if she would decorate their apartments. She told them that she couldn't make any promises; she would have to take a look first. And so she had five appointments for the following week and three more for the week after that to take a look first. And so she had five appointments for the following week and three more for the week after that. "I'm turning into a businesswoman," she said breathlessly. "Me, of all people! Can you imagine?"

Sorry, No Wrinkled Dollar Bills, Please

WHEN I WORKED AT TASS, I always dreaded payday. Since paychecks don't exist in Russia, people are paid in cash. Though it sounds like a nifty idea, there's a drawback: you have to stand in line. On the other hand, I got a lot of reading done this way. I finished Alice Walker's *In Love and Trouble* and Joseph Conrad's *Heart of Darkness*. One gray Monday morning I tucked a copy of *Anna Karenina* into my shoulder bag before heading over to the bookkeeper's office, which was in the building next door. When I arrived, about sixty people were waiting in the narrow corridor. Taking my place at the end of the line, I pulled out my book and plunged into it: "And then she thought how happy life might still be, and how tormentingly she loved and hated him. . . ." I turned the fragile, yellowing page carefully. "'Oh God! where am I to go?' she thought, walking further and further along the platform. She stopped at the end of it. . . . A goods train was approaching. . . ." My God, this was it, the big scene, Anna Karenina was about to throw herself in front of the train! Just then the man behind me sighed loudly, and I could feel his breath, which reeked of tobacco and whiskey, on my neck. Trying to ignore the smell, I read on. "Suddenly remembering the man who had been run over the day she first met Vronsky, she realized what she had to do. Quickly and lightly descending the steps. . .she stopped close to the passing train. . . .

"'There!' she said to herself. . . 'There, into the very middle, and I shall punish him and escape from everybody and from myself!'" At this point the man in back of me sneezed, and the tiny particles of saliva landed right on my neck. Just as I was wiping my neck with a tissue, the door opened and about a dozen people walked in. The line shifted a little to accommodate the newcomers. Suddenly a large foot was on top of mine. In agony, I dropped *Anna Karenina* on the floor. The man in front of me turned around. "Excuse me, I hope I didn't hurt you," he said, picking up my book and handing it to me. It was Igor, a senior editor I sometimes ran into in the elevator. I had been so absorbed in my reading that I had not noticed him.

"Thank you," I said, putting the book back into my shoulder bag.

"Don't mention it. What time do you have?"

"A quarter past eleven."

"Good Lord, we've been here for almost an hour!"

"Come on, hurry up," the bookkeeper, an old woman, yelled.

When it was finally Igor's turn, the woman, whose thin red hair was pulled back into a ponytail, handed him two five-thousand-ruble notes. "Don't forget to sign," she said, indicating a green ledger. Igor hurriedly scrawled his name. He then turned to me and said with a derisive laugh, "Sometimes I wonder why I even bother coming here. This money isn't worth squat. It's not backed by anything, not gold, not silver, not even bread."

That can't be true, I thought. It seemed extreme, even for Russia.

When my turn came, the bookkeeper handed me eight hundred rubles. I signed my name in Cyrillic, put the money in my wallet, and left.

It was raining, and I had forgotten to bring an umbrella. By the time I got back to the main building, I looked as though I had just taken a shower with my winter gear on. After slipping out of my jacket, I took off my boots and placed them by the radiator. Then I sat down at my wobbly wooden desk and began editing the pile of news stories that had been left there. But I couldn't get Igor's words out of my head. I had to know if what he said was true. So on my lunch hour I called Vyacheslav Aleksandrovich Zaslavsky, an economist at the Gorbachev Foundation. I didn't know him all that well; I had found his telephone number in my Rolodex. After a long pause he sighed and said, "It's true, all right."

"But how can that be?" I asked. Cradling the phone between my neck and shoulder, I pulled a one-thousand ruble note from my wallet and looked at the fine print. "It says right here that it's 'backed by gold, precious metals, and other assets of the State Bank.'"

"You Americans. Don't you realize that the government is full of shit?"

I felt like such a fool, a *durak* as Russians say. Rubles were worthless and everybody knew it except me. I suddenly understood what Russians meant by that old saying, "We pretend to work, and they pretend to pay us."

Things weren't always this bad, Vyacheslav Aleksandrovich assured me. In the late nineteenth century, rubles were backed by pure gold and could be exchanged in any bank for a gold coin. "People called them 'golden rubles,'" he said wistfully. "Ah, life was totally different back then. It's humiliating, what we are witnessing now. Such a great country, ruined."

I never knew how to respond to such sentiments, so I thanked him politely and told him that I needed to get back to work, which was true. Lyudmila was standing in front of me, waving a news story sent by our Prague correspondent. Printed at the top of the page was the word "urgent."

When I came home from work that evening, I turned on the television to watch *Field of Miracles*, a Russian version of *Let's Make a Deal*. Television was still controlled by the state, but programming was no longer limited to the best of Brezhnev (his old speeches) and the highlights of that year's potato harvest. Soap operas and game shows, which had never been broadcast before, were becoming popular, and I was curious about this new show.

A red velvet curtain parted, revealing the host, a pudgy, gray-haired man in a black tuxedo. "We're here to make miracles come true!" he boomed. Wading into the audience, he offered a grandmother from St. Petersburg a choice: twenty thousand rubles or a mystery prize in a shiny blue suitcase. He then told the man next to her, a scientist from Kharkov, that he could have forty thousand rubles or the unknown prize. Both contestants, who were each given thirty seconds to decide, chose the suitcase. "And what do we have inside?" the host asked, flashing an exaggerated grin. "Natasha, open it, please!" A drumroll played as the camera cut to a curvaceous blond in a sequined red evening gown, who opened the suitcase with a flourish of her rhinestone-braceleted wrist.

"And the treasure inside is . . . sixty thousand rubles!"

"Dammit!" said the scientist.

"Do we have to keep playing?" the grandmother asked with a sigh.

The host looked embarrassed. "We'll be right back," he said with an awkward smile. And the camera cut to a shiny red Volvo speeding down the highway, a woman's long blond hair streaming out of the window. "Volvo," said a deep male voice. "The choice of the modern generation."

This was in 1993, just one year after prices on all consumer goods were freed from state controls. Inflation had climbed to levels not seen in Russia since the chaos just before the Bolshevik Revolution, and the ruble was practically worthless. The grandmother and the scientist would surely have preferred the sleek red Volvo. Or a color television. Or even a cheap set of plastic dishes. Even an old pair of shoes would have been better than a suitcase full of rubles.

After the czar was deposed in 1917, the price of bread rose from a few kopecks to half a million rubles. Fearful that riots might break out, the provisional government raised salaries to at least ten million rubles a month. When payday came, people left offices and factories with bulging cloth sacks slung over their shoulders. That first year of market reform under Yeltsin, prices were once again so high that many people couldn't afford to buy enough food. Russian newspapers predicted that the economic chaos would lead to another revolution. And it did—but not the kind the political pundits had envisioned. As the ruble took a nose dive, many shopkeepers, mechanics, landlords, and even doctors began demanding dollars because they were seen as a more stable currency. A friend of mine, a filmmaker, told me the first thing actors who came for an audition said was, "Let's talk color. How are you going to pay me? In red or in green?" When he told them that he didn't have any *zeloniye*, or "green ones," as dollars were called, many of them walked right out of his small studio and never came back.

Making fun of the ruble turned into a national pastime. People called it "cabbage," perhaps because that was one of the cheapest vegetables available, or "wooden money."

"And the value of the wooden one has fallen again," newscasters would say when they announced the exchange rate over the radio. "As of this morning, one American dollar is worth six hundred of our wooden ones." Even children learned to mock the national currency. Svetlana's thirteen-year-old son, Kirill, once told me, "If you have fifteen or twenty rubles in your pocket, you may as well just throw them away."

Some of the new currencies that came after the ruble didn't command much respect either. Ukrainians called the tiny pink coupons that were issued after Ukraine won its independence in 1992, "*fantiki* [candy wrappers]." At a small, rocky beach in Koktybil, a remote village by the Black Sea, I saw people lying in the sun with the coupons folded over their noses. "Why not?" one of them said with a laugh when I asked him why he was wearing his country's currency on his nose. "I don't have any suntan lotion." In Lithuania people scoffed at their new currency, which was about the size of Monopoly money and was decorated with animal motifs, calling them "zoo tickets." Some of these new currencies turned out to be even more volatile than the "wooden one."

By the mid-1990s the ruble had more or less stabilized. But many people still had more confidence in the dollar. In fact, when the new one hundred dollar bill was introduced in 1996, the U.S. Treasury ran radio, television, and newspaper announcements in Russia and even set up a telephone help line that fielded more than one hundred calls a day. One Russian bank chartered a jet to bring the new bills back to Moscow as soon as they became available.

But Russians have their own rules about just what kind of bills they will accept. Those that are wrinkled, torn, or have anything written on them, even a stray pen mark, will not do. Why this obsession with perfection?

No one seems to know. Once, in a fit of pique, I asked the woman sitting behind the glass at a currency exchange point. (She had just refused to exchange fifty dollars because one of the bills had a barely discernible pen mark.) She thought that it might have something to do with the fact that less-than-perfect bills are not accepted in Turkey, where many Russian businessmen buy the goods they sell for a markup at home, but she wasn't sure. "How should I know?" she asked with a shrug. "Those are the rules. That's all I can tell you."

Frustrated, I called the Finance Ministry. "Why is it," I asked, "that no one in Russia will accept dollar bills that are slightly worn? Why do they have to look new?"

"*Chort yevo znayet*? Who the devil knows?" said one high-ranking ministry official. "Why do we still have a law against selling American dollars when they're sold on every corner? Why do we have to ask for humanitarian aid when we have some of the richest, most fertile land in the world? And how is it that we can send a man into space, but we can't develop a telephone system that works? At this moment I can hardly hear you. And I'm a deputy prime minister! My telephone is supposed to work!"

I should have known better than to expect a logical answer. Whenever I ventured to ask anyone about one of the many absurdities of post-Soviet life, I heard some variation of "This is Russia. What do you expect?"

A curious fact about currency exchange points: if they do accept imperfect dollars, they give you less than the full equivalent in rubles, in effect charging you for having untidy money. Knowing this, I tried to keep a supply of flawless bills on hand. I got them at the new, upscale banks that are reputedly run by the Russian mafia (ordinary state-run banks don't have dollars). Patronizing such banks can be risky. A group of armed men in black ski masks once raided the bank I usually went to. The police arrived on the scene and arrested the men, who turned out to be . . . members of President Boris Yeltsin's personal security service. They were all released immediately and none were taken to court. No official explanation was ever given. Reading about this episode in the newspaper, I was relieved that I had not run out of dollars *that* day.

There is one advantage to going to a commercial bank: the service tends to be good. Asking for new dollar bills is the one request that usually won't meet with a rude response because any teller working in one of those banks is likely to have a stash of dollars herself and knows very well that unless the bills are perfect, they are useless.

What do people do with all their wrinkled bills? Many of the Russians I knew ironed them to get the creases out. I kept mine between the pages of a book, like dried flowers. So, when my landlord called one morning to tell me that he would be coming over later that day to collect the rent in cash (personal checks aren't used), I went straight to my bookshelf and opened my brown, leather-bound copy of *Voina i Mir* [*War and Peace*]. Removing the blue satin ribbon that served as a bookmark, I inspected the five one hundred dollar bills and two tens I had placed there a few days ago in anticipation of Yura's visit. One of the ten dollar bills was still hopelessly wrinkled. I knew that if I gave it to Yura, who always examined each bill carefully, he would scowl and say, "This one is going to be a problem. Do you have another one?"

I resorted to the Russian method—I tried pressing the errant bill with my old-fashioned Soviet iron, which looked like an anvil and weighed about as much. But the creases were still visible, so I went to the bank to get a new ten dollar bill.

I gave the teller, a well-turned-out young woman in a black Chanel suit, my credit card and told her that I wanted a cash advance of one hundred dollars. But when she handed me the money, I noticed that one of the ten dollar bills was slightly wrinkled.

"Can you give me a nicer one?" I asked apologetically (no matter how often I did it, I still felt ridiculous asking someone to replace a wrinkled bill). "I don't mind personally; it's just that no one will accept a bill in this condition."

"I know, I know," she said, running a weary hand through her short, stylishly cut auburn hair. "But all I have are these." She held up a batch of ten dollar bills bound by a pink rubber band. From a distance they looked new, but when I took a closer look, I noticed a small slip of paper with something scrawled in blue ink: *nesoversheniye*, "imperfect."

"Hey, Yulia," the teller said, turning to the young woman at the next window, "do you have any fresh tens?"

"Sure, I've got a couple dozen," Yulia said, sliding the money under the glass.

As I walked out the door, cash in hand, I realized that the entire transaction had taken a mere fifteen minutes. So much had changed in just one year. I recalled a newspaper article written by an American, a corporate executive, who had tried to open a bank account in Moscow in 1992. Fearing that he would not get good service at a state-run bank, he decided to go to one of the sleek new commercial banks. Young, well-muscled guards stood in front of the glass doors with machine guns at the ready, a stark contrast to the frail old men who kept watch over ordinary banks, armed only with nightsticks. Inside the walls were bright pink and the furniture, all geometric shapes and angles, had obviously been imported. A sylph in a tight black miniskirt and matching stiletto heels gave the executive a ticket with a number on it and told him to watch a large electronic screen that resembled a scoreboard. It was ten o'clock. Two hours later, when his number finally flashed across the screen, he went to one of the windows and handed the teller a bag of money.

"I'd like to make a deposit," he said.

She opened the bag. "What's this?" she asked, pulling out a fistful of rubles. "You have to sort the money first."

SORRY, NO WRINKLED DOLLAR BILLS, PLEASE 117

"But there are three hundred million rubles in there. I'll be here all day."

"Well, *I'm* certainly not going to do it. You can use that table over there. Make sure you label each pile—fives, tens, twenties, and so on. And hurry up. We close in one hour."

"But the sign on the door says you're open till five."

"Yes, but we only take deposits until one. Why are you looking at me like that?"

"How can you—what kind of way is this to do—oh, never mind."

There was nothing for the executive to do but take off his jacket, roll up his sleeves, and start counting. By the time he was finished, it was nearly three o'clock. He would have to come back the next day. After it was all over, he wondered why he had bothered. "It would have been quicker for me to drive 180 kilometers out of Moscow to a secluded forest I know and bury the money," he wrote. "Even allowing for time to drive there and shovel, I figure I could have made three trips to dig up the cash and make partial withdrawals before spending the amount of time this single deposit cost me." (I had thought about opening a bank account, but when I found out that Russian banks didn't insure their customers' money, I wrapped my savings in newspaper and put it in the freezer instead. I figured the money was safer there, unless my apartment was burglarized by a hungry thief.)

Another American, also a corporate executive, with whom I struck up a conversation while standing in line at that same bank, asked me where commercial banks get all those perfect bills. I don't know. I'm curious myself. I do know that some banks throw away bills that have been torn and taped back together, and those that have a phone number or someone's musings scribbled in the corner—at least that's what one Russian bank manager told me. As for the rest of us, it was common practice to exchange such bills with someone traveling to "the civilized world," as Russians wistfully refer to any country outside the former Soviet Union, the idea being that he could use the imperfect currency wherever he was going (except Turkey, perhaps). Russians have a way of pulling together. No one I asked for such a favor ever refused. Even if the traveler was merely an acquaintance or even a stranger I met through a friend, there was a sense of camaraderie, a feeling that we were all in this together and had to help one another.

I was always on the lookout for innovative solutions to the wrinkled-dollar-bill problem. Everyone at my bank in Yonkers, New York, knew that when I came to make my annual withdrawal of about six thousand dollars, the bills had to look as though they had just rolled off the printing press. Supplying that many new bills was no easy task, since I also needed the money in small denominations, preferably twenties (for some reason, it's almost impossible to get change of large bills in Moscow). But this is no ordinary New York bank. About the size of a small studio apartment, it is filled with the aroma of fresh *blini* and the lively cadences of Ukrainian. The walls are covered with posters that remind patrons of the horrors of life under Communism. "Six Million Dead!" says one, referring to the Great Famine of 1932–33, when about that many Ukrainians starved to death as a result of Stalin's policy of forced collectivization. The bank is owned and operated entirely by Ukrainians; English is spoken only on those rare occasions when a non-Ukrainian speaker comes in (usually by mistake). My parents opened an account there when they first arrived in the United States in 1965 because they didn't trust American banks. "These are our people," my mother says. "We just felt more comfortable there." Growing up, I got to know all the tellers. I saw them in church every Sunday and at Ukrainian festivals and dances. After I moved to Moscow, they always asked my mother how I was doing "over there." Whenever I came in, they were excited to see me and nodded sympathetically when I complained about the outrageous practices of Russian exchange points, for example their frequent refusal to accept bills that were printed before 1988. One of those tellers, my next-door neighbor when I was growing up in Yonkers, even told me to call in advance to tell her exactly how much money I needed, so that she could have it ready for me when I came in.

* * *

Curiously, rubles were accepted everywhere, no matter what condition they were in. But Russia was changing so fast that using the national currency presented its own perils. In 1996 I took a brief trip to Madrid. When I returned to Moscow, I went to an exchange point inside the airport and handed the woman behind the counter fifty dollars. She gave me two hundred and fifty thousand rubles. As I held each bill up to the light to make sure that it wasn't counterfeit, an art I had never bothered to learn in the United States, I noticed something strange about the ten-thousand-ruble notes. Instead of the usual picture of the Kremlin's imposing towers set against an ultramarine background, these bills were green and had a drawing of some sort of canal amid mountains and treetops.

"They're new," said the woman.

"But I've only been out of the country for two weeks," I said.

"They were issued last Monday."

I thought of the three hundred thousand rubles (about sixty dollars) in my wallet. The bills were mostly ten-thou-sand-ruble notes. I wondered if they would be good for any-thing besides lining the bottom of my cat's litter box. "Have the old notes been withdrawn or are they still good?"

The woman shrugged. "Your guess is as good as mine."

The old notes were declared worthless—and had to be turned in within twenty-four hours. Lines outside banks stretched for miles. I drew solace from one thought: the mere fact that the government had issued new notes meant that the beleaguered ruble was finally making its way back into the economy.

Although no one ever called me an imperialist, I often felt like one. During the heyday of the economy's "dollarization," Russia resembled an American colony. Some privately owned shops accepted only dollars or other "hard" (exchangeable) currencies, such as German marks, French francs, and Japa-nese yen. Filled with exotic delights such as kiwis from New Zealand, Spanish ham, French chocolate cake—even corn flakes and Milky Way bars—these wonderlands of Western civilization began to appear shortly after the much-vaunted closing of the Beryozki, a chain of state-run shops that sold Western goods for hard currency. It seemed so hypocritical, all that high-flown talk about shutting down the Beryozki because they discriminated against ordinary Russians (only high-ranking party officials and foreigners were allowed inside). Were the new hard currency shops any better? Theoretically anyone could shop at the *valutniye magazini*—here there were no guards demanding to see identification at the door. But the reality was that most people couldn't buy anything because they didn't have any hard currency.

Only the post-Soviet jet set could afford to go there, and shopping at such stores soon became what going to dinner at McDonald's once was—a sign of wealth, power, and status. Well-coiffed women came in their most glamorous evening clothes, even during the day, and bought the most expensive items: fresh salmon at $30 a pound, $150 bottles of champagne, dainty boxes of Godiva chocolates for $50, and fresh strawberries, imported from Holland, at $12 a basket. They loaded everything into large carts, which were conveniently provided by the shop, and waited in the briefest of lines. Salesclerks briskly rang up their purchases on modern cash registers, instead of relying on ancient abacuses. And then came the ultimate moment of triumph: the women paid for it all with crisp $100 bills drawn from elegant little Gucci bags by bejeweled hands.

Ordinary Russians flocked to the hard currency stores out of curiosity. They walked slowly up and down the aisles, admiring the shelves of beautifully packaged goods. They were careful not to touch anything and often admonished their children if they dared to pick anything up, as though they were in a museum filled with priceless artifacts.

Once, while shopping inside the Irlansky Dom Na Arbatye "Irish House on the Arbat," one of the first hard currency stores, I saw an old woman grab a shopping cart and begin hurriedly filling it. The cart was almost full when she noticed the strange symbol—a dollar sign—next to the prices. "*Devushka*," she said to me, "These prices, are they in rubles?" I explained (rather guiltily) that the prices were in dollars. The woman looked at the cart full of food. "Well," she said, "I guess that there is nothing for an ordinary person like me to do in this store." She left the cart right there, in the middle of the aisle, and stormed out.

By the mid-1990s hard currency stores were required by law to accept either rubles or hard currency. But store managers found a loophole. Arguing that the dollar was still stronger than the ruble—it crashed several times on the Moscow Interbank Currency Exchange in the early 1990s—they began setting their own inflated exchange rates to offset potential losses. So, if a Russian who had only rubles and an American with dollars each wanted to buy a can of soda that cost $2.00, the American would pay the regular price while the Russian would have to pay, say, six thousand rubles—the equivalent of $2.40. Or maybe even more. It all depended on the store and the exchange rate the manager had decided on. In the end, most Russians were forced to continue shopping at the poorly stocked but considerably cheaper state stores.

It eventually became illegal for businesses to accept payment in hard currency. Everything was to be sold for rubles only. It took no less than a presidential decree to bring about this long-overdue change. Although the ruble crashed again in 1998, merchants are not supposed to accept dollars (or any other hard currency). But many people now work for private companies, many of which pay their employees in dollars. Others, mostly women who were let go by state enterprises struggling to cut costs in the new market economy, have begun small, home-run businesses that bring them a modest dollar income. For this growing new segment of the population, known as the "dollar generation," the rubles-only law is merely a nuisance. It's also inconvenient for foreigners, since most of them are paid in dollars, as I was after I left TASS and started writing full-time for American and European newspapers.

One cloudy afternoon I was walking down a narrow street covered with ice. A light snow was falling. Bundled-up *babushki* were sitting on wooden crates, hawking Reeboks, children's winter jackets, Sony television sets, flowers, homemade cheeses, and necklaces of dried mushrooms. "*Pokupaite! Pokupaite!*" they shouted. I kept walking until I noticed that one of them was holding a shiny new toaster in her gloved hands. My toaster had literally gone up in smoke the week before. So I stopped.

"How much?" I asked.

"Five hundred thousand," she replied.

I considered haggling but thought better of it. *Take it or leave it*, the expression on her deeply lined face seemed to say.

Quickly I calculated how much money I would need to exchange—$103. I checked my wallet. All I had were two $10 bills. So, I caught a trolleybus back to my apartment and took $83 out of the freezer. After checking all the bills to make sure that there were no pen marks or wrinkles, I went to an exchange point to convert them into rubles. It was closed. CLEANING DAY, the sign on the window said. I tried another one. Same problem. Finally I found one that was open. Rubles in hand, I went back to the *babushka* and bought the toaster. All of this took two and a half hours.

I probably should have asked her if I could pay her in dollars. Having run the gauntlet of *babushki* at many bazaars, I had noticed that some of them wore aprons with big pockets filled with dollars. Others were more discreet, stuffing the dollars into their satchels. Watching these savvy *babushki*, it was hard to believe that not so long ago, street vendors were afraid to accept dollars because they were contraband. When I unwittingly offered a vendor five dollars in 1991, he looked as though I had just handed him a rattlesnake. "What kind of money is that?" he asked. "Are those dollars?" I told him they were. "It's not allowed," he said, moving away from me. "They could throw me in jail for that. Go! Get out of here, I beg of you, before someone sees us."

But the influx of dollars did more than change the face of business. It profoundly altered people's attitudes toward money. When my printer broke in 1994, I called Oleg, a computer programmer who repaired printers on the side. By then prices seemed to be rising every hour, and everyone was searching for ways to *podrabativat*, make fast money. So I wasn't surprised when Oleg offered to come to my apartment that very evening. I wondered how much he would charge me, but when he was finished, he picked up his toolbox, put on his coat, and headed for the door without a word.

"Wait, how much do I owe you?" I asked.

"You don't owe me anything," he said.

I pulled a twenty-dollar bill out of my wallet and handed it to him, but he blushed and refused to take it. When I pressed him—I told him that he deserved to be paid for his labor—he bowed his head low, as if in shame, and finally agreed to accept five dollars. "Thank you, thank you," he said, still blushing.

I called Oleg again in the spring of 1997, when my computer suddenly came down with a mysterious virus. He corrected the problem and unceremoniously informed me that I owed him fifty dollars for two hours of work—about two weeks' worth of wages for the average Russian worker. Was this the same Oleg? "I would prefer two twenties and a ten, if you don't mind," he said as he put on his big fur hat and buttoned his jacket. "It's so hard to get change of a fifty. Oh, and please, new bills only. I don't want any wrinkled ones."

The Washing Machine that Needed Time to Rest

I WANTED a washing machine. But it was 1992, and all my coworkers at TASS said that buying a washing machine—even a used one—was a chimera. "Who put such a foolish notion into your head?" one of them asked me. "Even if you do find one, what will you use to wash the clothes? There's no detergent to buy." Even one of my American colleagues exuded nothing but dour pessimism when I told her of my plan. "You know what your trouble is?" she asked me one day. "You keep thinking you're going to get one. I *know* that it's hopeless, and I've accepted it."

I had been in Moscow for nearly two months and all I had done, it seemed, was go to work, shop for food (an endless task in itself), and do the laundry. My back ached from bending over a bathtub full of dirty clothes every Saturday night. The skin on my hands was dry and cracked from too much exposure to detergent and hot water, and my fingers were sore from washing and wringing out all those heavy winter clothes. The entire process, including hanging everything up to dry, took about four hours. I often felt exhausted. But the piles of dirty laundry, which I kept in the two big red suitcases I had brought from New York, kept growing. I was getting desperate.

Leaving my apartment to go to work one cloudy Monday morning, I pressed the elevator button. After about five minutes, I realized that the elevator, as often happens in Russian buildings, wasn't working, a major inconvenience since I lived on the twelfth floor. I dashed down the stairs, my footsteps echoing in the dingy building. When I reached the eleventh floor, I heard the sound of keys jangling.

"*Dobroe utro.* Good morning," said my friend Sasha. She was trying to lock her front door while holding her baby daughter, who was wrapped in a fluffy pink blanket. The baby's tiny fist poked out of the blanket. She squealed with delight as she tried to grab the shiny silver keys from her mother's hand.

"*Dobroe utro,*" I said. "You look as though you could use some help."

"Thanks," she said, handing me the keys. "The big one is for the top lock, and the smaller one is for the bottom."

"How's it going?" I asked as I locked the door.

"The same as always—busy. I'm off to the park with Mashenka. Then I'll leave her with my mother—thank God for Mama—and go pick up some groceries. After that I have to do the laundry. Between the kids, Volodya, and Mama, I've got plenty of clothes to wash."

I gave the keys back to her, and she put them in her handbag.

"I don't know how you manage," I said. "I don't think I could do it."

"Oh, it's not so bad. I have a washing machine."

"I know. I noticed it in your bathroom the other night. Where did you get it?"

"My parents gave it to me as a wedding present when I got married five years ago. Why? Are you looking for one?"

"Actually I am."

"I haven't seen any in a long time."

"Do you have any connections? Do you know anyone who works in a shop?"

"No, unfortunately, I don't. Why don't you just go to a laundry service? There's one near Pushkin Square."

A laundry service! Of course. Why hadn't I thought of that?

"There's just one thing. There are a few rules."

Somehow I knew there would be rules.

"They won't take anything with zippers or buttons. Well, you can give them things with buttons, but you have to cut them off beforehand. You can sew them on again after you get your laundry back. They're pretty quick. They generally take about three weeks. Oh, and make sure you don't give them anything you really care about—they might ruin it."

But Sasha hadn't been to the *prachechnaya* in a long time. "Maybe the rules have changed," she said hopefully. I thought of calling and asking about the button-and-zipper rule, but Sasha didn't have the number. If only there were telephone books in Moscow! Since she didn't know the exact address, I couldn't call Information either. I resolved to go downtown to look for the place.

"Well, thanks for the idea," I said. "What time is it?"

"Ten after eight."

"I'd better get going or I'll miss the bus. *Dosvidanya!*"

I went on to face the day with a renewed sense of optimism. Soon, I thought, I'll be free from the drudgery of washing clothes by hand.

Sasha had always been kind to me. I met her my first week in Moscow. I had boarded a bus at the stop in front of our building. Everyone entered through the back door and inserted little white tickets into a small red machine that was attached to the side of the bus, just above the windows. I didn't have a ticket and looked around nervously. But the driver was busy steering the bus through the morning traffic and, as far as I could tell, no one else cared whether I had paid the fare or not. I didn't know then that plainclothes policemen sometimes ask passengers to produce their tickets, and that anyone caught without one must pay a fine and get off the bus immediately. I was standing by the window when a tall young woman, who was holding a baby wrapped in a pink blanket, asked me if I had a ticket.

"I didn't know that I needed one," I replied. "I've never taken a bus in Moscow before."

"Where are you from?" she asked.

"New York."

"Oh! You're American."

"Can I buy a ticket from the driver?"

"No, you can only get them at metro stations. Here, take one of mine," she said, pulling a ticket out of her wallet.

I tried to pay her, but she refused to take any money.

"*Nye nado*. It's not necessary," she said. And then, in heavily accented English, "You are guest in my country. Let it be as my gift to you. My English is not so good, but you understand, yes?"

Such solicitude toward foreigners was an endearing trait I had noticed in many Russians. When Sasha and I discovered that we were neighbors, I invited her over for dinner and we became friends.

Although we were about the same age, Sasha watched over me with an almost maternal fervor. Whenever we went for a stroll, she would link her arm firmly through mine— she was afraid I might slip on the ice. "No, not there," she would admonish as she steered me past a particularly treacherous spot. Sometimes she scolded me for walking too quickly, and once she even retied my scarf. Often, when we returned from such excursions, we would go to Sasha's apartment and feast on homemade goose soup and *pyelmyeni*, delectable ravioli-size dumplings filled with beef. Occasionally she baked cookies shaped like little snowmen and gave me a couple dozen to take home. Butter and flour were virtually impossible to find, making her gift all the more precious.

The following Saturday I rose early and dressed quickly. Pulling the heavy suitcases, I lumbered through the snow. Both suitcases were equipped with wheels, but I had crammed so many dirty clothes into them that they kept tipping over, and I had to stop every few feet to restore them to an upright position. Perspiring heavily, I took off my scarf and unbuttoned my coat. Finally, I made it to the metro station, where I took a trolleybus to Pushkin Square. After wandering around for about an hour, I came to a small storefront. I tried to look inside, but the windows were covered with frost. There was no sign. Could this be the *prachechnaya*? I opened the door. There, in the middle of a shabby room, was what looked to be a stupendous washing machine: it was about six feet high; I had never seen anything like it. The stale air reeked of wet wool and disinfectant. The floor was filthy, and cockroaches the size of dragonflies were crawling on the walls. My first impulse was to leave immediately. But I was curious why there was only this one huge machine and how it worked. I decided to ask the portly attendant, who explained, rather curtly, that this was no longer a laundry service. It was now a *khimchistka*, a dry cleaner's, and they accepted only coats and jackets.

I caught a trolleybus back to the metro station, then took the bus to my apartment. The elevator was out of order again, so I had to drag the suitcases up twelve flights of stairs. When I finally reached the twelfth floor, my back was sore and my arms ached. Panting, I threw open the door to my apartment, put the suitcases down, and staggered into bed. I was soon fast asleep. When I awoke, about an hour later, I remembered that Jennifer, an American copy editor at TASS, had invited me to her party. Feeling weary and downcast, I considered staying home, but I had already told her that I would come.

When I arrived at Jennifer's three-room apartment, the lights were low and "Hey, Jude," her favorite song, was playing on the stereo. People were sipping juice and munching on a variety of *zakuski*: enormous platters of salted fish and salami; slices of white bread smothered with butter and red and black caviar; boiled eggs; and a salad made of radishes, cucumbers, beets, and cabbage. I helped myself to some salted fish and asked a few women if they had seen any washing machines lately. Asking such a question at a party is not as strange as it may sound. The price and availability of consumer goods is a popular topic of conversation in Russia, particularly among women, who do most of the shopping.

But trying to track down a washing machine was a little like investigating a UFO—it wasn't hard to find someone who had seen one, but everyone was a little fuzzy on the details. Mostly they showed me callused hands, rough and red from years of washing clothes in the bathtub.

"My mother had one," said one woman wistfully. "Of course, that was almost fifteen years ago; my husband and I were still newlyweds. It worked pretty well for about a year; then it broke down. We called a repairman and he managed to fix it—he had golden hands, that man. We used it for a couple of months or so, but then it went on the fritz again. I've been using these ever since." She held out her hands and wiggled her fingers. "My husband says they work just as well," she said with an acrid laugh.

Lyuba, a young schoolteacher with a bouffant hairdo and heavy makeup, looked at me sympathetically and said, "They're very hard to find nowadays. I did see one in a shop over on Leninski Prospekt."

"Do you remember the address?" I asked eagerly. "What was the name of the shop?" I fumbled around in my handbag for a piece of paper and a pen.

"I don't know. It was about six months ago. Or maybe it was on Kutuzovsky Prospekt. . . ." She thought for a moment and then said, "I'm sorry. I just can't remember. But

they're so expensive! I've never had one and I have a husband and two small children. You live alone, you say? Are
you sure you need one?"

I stared at her in utter amazement. "I definitely need
one. Washing clothes by hand takes too much time."

"Poor thing. You're not used to our way of life. I wish I
could help you." She glanced down at my nearly empty plate.
"Would you like some more fish?"

"I could go for some more."

"*Paidyomte.* Let's go," said Lyuba, leading the way back
to the buffet table in the living room. "That's strange," she
remarked. "Someone turned off the lights in there." She
found the switch and turned it on. In a corner of the room a
middle-aged man was pawing a young girl on the sofa. The
girl, who was perhaps seventeen or eighteen, looked at us
with startled eyes. She quickly got up and left the room,
clutching her silky white blouse, which was almost completely unbuttoned. Lyuba's eyes followed her willowy figure.
"Fedya," she said to the man, with a nervous little laugh,
"what are you up to, scaring young girls like that?" The
man's eyes were glassy, his lips twisted in a crooked smile.
His hand was so unsteady that he spilled his drink, forming
a little pool of vodka around his shoe. "You'll ruin your
shoes!" Lyuba said in the beseeching tone of a mother wiping the mouth of a drooling child. She took a napkin from
the buffet table, got down on her knees, and started wiping
his shoes. She then got some more napkins and began cleaning up the mess on the floor. "It's better to do it right away
before the stain sets in," she said to me. "Would you move
that chair a little? That's good. Thanks. That man is so clumsy

sometimes. He's worse than the children." My God, I thought, *this* guy is her husband?

I talked with a few other women that night, but none of them had any idea where I might find a washing machine. They advised me to abandon my quest. "Be happy that you're still single," said one tired-looking woman. "One day you'll marry, and you'll have even more laundry to do." I went home thinking that maybe buying a washing machine was a pipe dream after all.

About a month later, Ivan, a young editor at TASS, graciously offered to go shopping with me. (Ivan had told me he was married, and I understood that he was offering to help me merely because I was a foreigner.) We met in the metro on a rainy Sunday morning and spent the whole day going from one virtually empty shop to another. By nightfall we were hungry, so I suggested that we go to Pizza Hut. Taking him out to dinner was the least I could do, I thought, to repay him for his kindness.

Inside the restaurant everything looked clean and new. The walls were freshly painted a pistachio green, and on the tables were white linen tablecloths and delicate vases filled with red and white carnations.

"Good evening," said a well-groomed waiter. "Table for two?"

"Yes," I said.

He led us to a small table next to a window. "Will this be satisfactory?"

"This will be fine, thank you," I replied. He smiled and pulled out a chair for me. He then handed us two menus. "*Priyatnava apetita.* Enjoy your meal."

"What do you feel like having?" I asked Ivan.

"Nothing, I'll just keep you company," he said, looking a little uneasy. "I've never been in a place like this. It's so cozy. What does pizza taste like?"

"It's good. Try it."

"There are so many," he said, looking at the colorful laminated menu, which listed twelve different kinds of pizza, including "Russian pizza," which came with slices of *kolbasa*, a type of sausage. "I can't make up my mind."

Ivan finally decided on the Hawaiian pizza, which was topped with slices of fresh pineapple, and a Coke. I had an "American pizza" (no toppings, just tomato sauce and cheese) and a Sprite. When we were ready to leave, I signaled to the waiter, who walked briskly to our table.

"Yes, madam? Will there be anything else?"

"No, thank you. We're ready for the check."

He placed the bill in front of Ivan and looked at him expectantly. When I handed the waiter a twenty-dollar bill, he glanced at Ivan with an amused expression and promised to return in a moment with the change. Ivan looked mortified.

Later that evening I told Sasha what I had done.

"Of course he was upset," she said. "You shamed him. In this country women *never* treat men."

"What about birthdays or name days?"

"Even then. A woman may bake a cake or give the man flowers, but *under no circumstances* would she take him out for a meal."

Sasha told me that there was no such thing as going Dutch either.

Obviously I had a lot to learn.

Ivan and I sometimes ate lunch together, but the next day he avoided me. We did pass each other in the lobby once. I considered apologizing, but he looked so embarrassed when he saw me, I figured the less said about the previous evening, the better. Sitting alone at my desk reading the *Moscow Guardian*, an English-language newspaper, while munching on a ham sandwich, I spotted an intriguing advertisement: "Native Muscovite willing to be your guide, assistance of all kinds. Call 663-2078."

I dialed the number. The man who answered gave only his first name, Aleksandr. "That's all you need to know," he said. Aleksandr was soft-spoken and sounded a bit timid. He seemed nervous. I told him that I needed a washing machine. He asked me how much I was willing to pay. I thought about the two suitcases of dirty laundry. They were so full that I couldn't even close them anymore. I told him that I would pay him ten dollars, which was a lot of money in 1992, if he found a machine by Friday (it was Monday), twenty dollars if he found one by Wednesday. I explained that I wanted a *polniy avtomat*—an automatic machine with a spin cycle. (Most washing machines were little more than rubber basins with small plastic propellers that looked as if they had been taken from a child's toy helicopter.)

Aleksandr said that he would have to make a few calls. About an hour later the telephone rang. "I have a machine for you," he said.

"How much?" I asked.

"He says he can't discuss the price over the phone. He wants you to meet him at Metro Shukinskaya tomorrow at five o'clock. He'll be in a yellow car."

"I'll be there. Can you give me some idea how much money I should bring?"

"One hundred dollars should be enough, but bring more just in case. When do I get paid?"

"When I bring the machine home and see that it works."

"That's not acceptable."

I apologized and explained that I just didn't feel comfortable paying him up front. Aleksandr insisted that I was being unreasonable, then grudgingly agreed to my terms.

I wanted that washing machine, but I wasn't willing to risk my life to get it. So, after I hung up, I called Volodya, Sasha's tall and muscular husband, and his nephew Aleksei. The next day the three of us piled into Aleksei's beat-up Moskvich and drove to metro Shukinskaya. We arrived ten minutes early. At exactly five o'clock a yellow car pulled up behind us. Inside we could see a man with a gray fur hat that was so big it nearly covered his eyes; he kept looking furtively in the rearview mirror. We walked over to the car.

"Are you the man with the washing machine?" Volodya asked.

The man eyed Volodya warily. "*Da.*"

Volodya shook his hand and introduced himself. The man stared at us with small blue eyes. His long, thin nose protruded from his face like a beak.

"Well, where is it?" asked Aleksei.

"Follow me."

We followed the little yellow car into a dense forest filled with snow-covered birch trees. "I don't think I like this," I said nervously. "Where is he taking us?"

Aleksei was busy weaving through the trees and trying to avoid the rocks. His hands gripped the steering wheel so tightly that I could see the veins. "Who the hell knows? Should I follow him or not?"

"Keep going," I said.

As we drove deeper into the forest, all the trees began to look alike. How will we ever find our way out of here? I wondered.

The car came to a stop just outside a garage. The man got out and opened the door. Inside were four cars (three Soviet-made Ladas and some kind of foreign car that had been painted bright red), some Japanese stereo equipment, and three washing machines.

The man, who still hadn't told us his name, picked up one of the washing machines and set it down in front of me.

"The money," he said gruffly.

"Just a minute," I said. "I want to take a look at the machine."

He looked irritated.

"How can I buy it without taking a look at it first?"

He opened the box and took the machine out. It was small (about three feet high) and white.

"Is it new?" I asked, opening the lid and peering inside.

He didn't answer.

"Does it work?"

"Of course."

"Can you plug it in so I can see for myself?"

"No."

"How can I be sure that it works?"

"You can't."

It was obvious that he was not going to accommodate me. Why should he? He was a black marketeer, after all, not a department store salesman. Take it, I thought. This is your only chance.

"How much do you want for it?"

"One hundred dollars."

I handed him a crisp one-hundred-dollar bill. He held it up to the light and inspected it carefully before stuffing it into his coat pocket. Without another word he closed the garage door and drove off. We stood there and watched until the little yellow car disappeared into the forest.

I took the washing machine home. After studying the instructions carefully, I felt confident enough to use it. I did one load. It took three hours, but everything went smoothly. So I put another load in. Midway through the rinse cycle, I heard a loud noise. When I got to the kitchen, water was gushing out of the machine with such force that the lid nearly came off its hinges. I yanked the plug out of the wall and ran to the bathroom to get a mop. Just then the doorbell rang. It was Sasha. She was holding some towels.

"There's water coming down my living room wall," she said matter-of-factly. "I figured that it must be coming from your apartment."

"I'm really sorry," I said. "I bought a washing machine, and it overflowed."

"Where is it?"

"In the kitchen."

"Good Lord," said Sasha, surveying the three-inch flood. "Well, we'd better get to it. We've got a lot of work to do." She took off her shoes and socks, waded into the soapy water, and began wiping it up with the towels she had brought.

By the time we finished, about four hours later, it was nearly ten o'clock. I made us some tea and toast and brought it into the living room. With our jeans still rolled up, we sat on the sofa and put our feet on an old black trunk that I used as a coffee table.

"Thanks so much for helping me," I said. "I'm really sorry about the damage to your wall. I'll pay for it."

"That's all right," she said. "These things happen. It wasn't your fault." She looked at her watch. "I really should be getting back. I have to give the kids a bath and put them to bed. Mama's not home—she's working the night shift at the factory—and Volodya can't manage it all by himself. Do me a favor, will you?"

"Sure, what is it?"

"Don't do any more laundry, at least not tonight."

"Don't worry," I said with a sheepish grin, "I won't."

After Sasha left I washed the dishes with shampoo (dishwashing detergent was scarce) and plopped on the sofa. Still holding a soapy sponge, I had intended merely to sit down for a moment. But I was so exhausted that I fell asleep, still in my clothes. The next morning the sponge was on the carpet and my back was so sore that I could hardly move. By this time, everyone at the office had heard that I had bought a washing machine.

"*Pozdravlayu!* Congratulations!" said my boss, Aleksandr Sergeyevich Nechayev.

"Thanks," I said feebly.

"Well, you did it," said Larissa, an austere-looking translator who always wore her thin, dark hair in a chignon. "I don't know *how* you did it, but I'm glad you finally found one. What's the matter?" she asked, seeing the look on my face. "I thought you'd be happy."

"I've been duped," I said.

"What do you mean?"

I told her about the flood.

"What kind of washing machine did you buy?"

"An Evrika Avtomat," I said, naming a well-known brand.

"Really? I have an Evrika and it works just fine. How many loads did you do?"

"Two."

"After you did the first load, how long did you wait before you put the next one in?"

"I did the second load as soon as the first one was done. Why would I wait?"

She shook her head. "*Vot gde sabaka ryta*! That's where the dog is buried!" she said, repeating a popular Russian expression. "You have to give the machine time to rest."

"*Time to rest?*"

"You're supposed to wait fifteen minutes in between loads," she explained patiently. "Our washing machines are like Soviet workers. When they perform a task, they need to take a break. You can't expect too much from things that were simply not designed to work well."

Larissa's appraisal of Russian washing machines did not surprise me. I noticed that people often spoke of locally produced goods in disparaging tones. Russia, as a nation, has low self-esteem. A person in a shop will often point to a frying pan or television and ask the salesclerk, "Was this made in our country?" If the response is "Yes," the shopper will probably retort, "Then it can't be any good. Do you have any imported ones?"

Anything foreign—even a candy bar—is revered and treated as something precious. Since Snickers is Sasha's favorite candy bar (Twix and Snickers are sold on virtually every street corner), I would sometimes bring her one when she invited me to her apartment for dinner. She would peel the wrapper off carefully, put it on one of her best plates, and cut it up into little slices. The Snickers bar would sit there, in the middle of the dinner table, like a tiny cake. She and Volodya would each take one piece and leave the rest for their two toddlers, Alyosha and Vyera. I never saw anyone treat a Russian candy bar with such tender ritualism.

Imported goods confer a certain cachet, but people prefer them for another reason. They tend to be of better quality than goods produced in Russia, although they are also much more expensive and many people can't afford them. Being of modest means, I, too, generally bought Russian brands. Although I often regretted doing so, some Russian-made goods, like my washing machine, for instance, proved to be of better quality than I expected. To be sure, the flood in my kitchen was only the beginning of my troubles. Within the first three months I had to call a repairman four times. Even on good days the machine jumped up and down and squeaked, and when it was going through the spin cycle, it rocked and shook so much that it moved several feet. I was sure it wouldn't last a year. But it was still working when I decided to leave Moscow in 1997, and my friend Margarita, a retired scientist who lives on a small pension, asked me if I wouldn't mind giving it to her. One summer evening not long ago, I called her from New York. To my surprise Margarita reported that the machine was still going strong.

"It's an absolute dream," she told me. "It's made my life so much easier."

"I'm curious," I said. "How long do you let it 'rest' between loads?"

"Oh, not long," she said. "A half hour or so."

All the Clean Ones Are Married

I WAS HAVING TEA with Lena and her husband, Seryozha, in their tiny apartment when the doorbell rang. Lena put down her tea cup and went to see who it was. "Boris! *Privyet!* Here, let me take your coat. Have you had dinner yet?"

"Actually I haven't eaten anything since lunch."

"Well, sit down. We're having chicken with fried potatoes *and* I've got a *chocolate* cake in the oven."

"Chocolate cake? Well, that settles it."

Boris took off his boots, which were wet from the snow, and followed Lena into the living room. "Lori, I'd like you to meet Seryozha's brother."

"*Privyet,*" I said.

He smiled shyly and sat down in a chair at the other end of the table, across from me. His face wasn't handsome, but I liked it. His brown eyes were big and round and innocent-looking. His cheeks were bright pink from the cold, and his hair, which was blond, was sticking up a little; it was a bit staticky from the wool hat he had been wearing. I guessed that he was about thirty-five, but he seemed younger somehow. Maybe it was his awkwardness. He didn't say anything, although he did look up and smile every now and then.

Lena disappeared into the kitchen. I could hear pots and pans clanging. After about five minutes Seryozha called out, "Hey, Lena, what's going on in there? We're waiting."

"I'm coming, I'm coming."

Lena came out of the kitchen with a large, steaming pot and put it on the table. She then turned on the television so that we could watch the news while we ate. The main story that evening was a summit meeting between President Boris Yeltsin and Leonid Kravchuk, the president of Ukraine. Yeltsin's gait was unsteady as he walked across the Kremlin's red carpet and extended a hearty, hail-fellow hand to Kravchuk. When he turned to the camera, he looked disoriented. The reporter standing next to him had to repeat her question twice. Roused from his stupor, Yeltsin spoke haltingly, slurring his words.

"God, look at him," Boris remarked. "He looks just like a common village drunk, an old grandpa who doesn't give a damn about anything but the bottle."

"Does Clinton drink?" Lena asked me.

"I'm sure he does," I answered, "but not to this extent, at least not in public."

"Would it bother you if he got drunk in public?" Seryozha wanted to know.

"Well, it would be kind of embarrassing if he was so plotzed that he couldn't get off the plane to go meet a prime minister," I replied, thinking of the time that a plastered Yeltsin could not be persuaded to get out of his plane in Shannon, Ireland, where the Irish prime minister and an official delegation were waiting.

"In America that would be a huge scandal," Boris observed. "But here it's different. Don't forget where we are living, Lori. People in this country would not approve of Yeltsin if he didn't drink. They would say that he wasn't a real man."

"Remember all the flak Gorbachev got?" said Seryozha, referring to the former president's deeply unpopular anti-alcohol campaign in 1986, when vodka was rationed to two bottles a month per family. (He renounced the measure in 1988.)

"Well, drunk or not, I think Yeltsin's doing a good job," Lena declared. Not so long ago she and Seryozha, a poet, had thought about emigrating to Israel. They could have— Lena is half Jewish. But they abandoned the idea after Yeltsin became president. "Why would we want to leave now? We have all the freedom we could ask for. As for the economic situation, it's certainly not perfect, but it's much better than it was five or seven years ago, when there was nothing at all in the shops. Really, Borya, what difference does it make if he has a little nip now and then? It's normal."

"You see," Boris said, turning to me, "it's just as I told you."

"Have you heard the one about Yeltsin and the ditch?" Seryozha asked us.

"No," I said, "let's hear it."

"Yeltsin is stumbling along a village road and falls into a ditch. A farmer passes by and sees him lying there, moaning. He grabs the president by the arm and pulls him out. 'Thank you, thank you, my good man,' Yeltsin says, brushing the mud from his suit. 'Please do me a favor: don't tell anyone that I fell into a ditch.' 'On one condition,' says the farmer. 'If you don't tell anyone that I pulled you out.'"

After the meal Lena brought out the cake, still warm from the oven, and brewed some more tea in an antique silver samovar. We all had at least one piece of the moist, satisfying dessert and several cups of tea. Before we knew it, it was almost eleven o'clock.

"Lori, I can't allow you to go home by yourself at this hour," Lena said firmly. "You can spend the night in Grisha's room. He can sleep in our bed."

"Don't worry, Lenochka," Boris said. "I'll walk Lori home."

"Oh, well, in that case—thank you, Borya."

Lena was always anxious about my safety. I was a little apprehensive myself. To get to my apartment I had to take the metro to Kievsky train station, which was filled with drunks. Sometimes there were Gypsies, too, and they often robbed people. So Lena and I had a little ritual: I would call her as soon as I got home just to let her know that I was all right. If the metro got rerouted (because of track work), and the trip took a little longer than usual, there would be a message on my answering machine: "Lori, this is Lena. I'm wondering where you are. Please call me when you get in, no matter how late it is."

That night Lena hugged Boris and me and playfully shooed us out the door. "Go, go, scoot!" A moment later, the door opened again. "Borya," she called out as we walked down the dark, narrow stairwell. "Make sure you see her all the way into the elevator!"

"I will!"

The night air was cold and it was drizzling, so Boris and I put on our hoods. As we made our way to my apartment, he told me about his job as an interpreter for a Swedish pharmaceutical company. "They needed someone so badly that they were willing to take me," he quipped. "The interviewer said, 'Say something in Swedish.' I said, 'My name is Boris,' and he said, 'You're hired.'" I was charmed by his sense of humor. I also discovered that we shared a common love of Russian literature. So, when he called a few months later and asked if I would like to see Nikita Mikhailkov's new film, *Burnt by the Sun*, I said I would be delighted. He had wanted to call me sooner, he explained, but he was shy and nervous around women. "'What if she says no?' I kept asking Lena. 'Just grab the goose by the beak,' she told me, but I couldn't. She finally dialed your number and handed me the receiver."

We decided to meet on a warm Saturday afternoon in June. I had just slipped into my new summer dress when I heard the familiar chorus of birds—my doorbell. I applied a touch of pink lip gloss, sprayed some perfume on my neck, and hurried to the door. "*Privyet.*"

Nothing could have prepared me for the shock I got when I saw Boris. His hair was greasy and full of big dandruff flakes, which were also visible on his black sweater, and when he said, "How nice to see you again," I got a whiff of his foul breath. Had there been a diplomatic way out, I would surely have taken it. Since there wasn't, I put on a sweater, grabbed my handbag, and locked the door behind me, hoping that I didn't look as disappointed as I felt.

The Moskva Theater was hot and stuffy. I took off my sweater and put it on the empty seat to my right. Boris removed his pullover and handed it to me. It was obvious that the sweater, which smelled like a butcher's garbage can, hadn't been washed in many months. I shuddered at the thought of touching it, much less putting it on top of my own sweater, but I didn't want to offend him, so I did. Although I put it on the edge of the seat—far away from me— I could smell it throughout the movie.

We took the metro home. It was jam-packed, and we had to stand by the doors, our bodies pressed up against one another. Boris, who was a few inches taller than me, spoke right into my face and I was overwhelmed by his breath, which smelled even worse after the pickled mushroom and liverwurst sandwich he had just eaten (we stopped at a refreshment stand after the movie). If only I could put some distance between us, but I couldn't move an inch. There were several people in front of us, including a huge woman clutching a bag of potatoes and a thin man holding a guitar in one hand and a baby in the other. As the metro whizzed through the city, jostling us to and fro, I tried not to breathe through my nose. It was a little like taking swimming lessons. That's it, I thought, take a deep breath, now exhale. *You can do this.*

We got off at Kievsky station and walked to my apartment. When we reached my door, Boris took a step forward and looked at me the way men do when they want to kiss a woman. I told him that I felt nauseous—which was true— and that I needed to lie down.

"I had no idea you were feeling sick," he said, with a look of concern. "Tea soothes the stomach, you know. You should have some before you go to bed."

"That's a good idea," I replied. "I will." Feeling guilty, I thanked him for an enjoyable evening, and we chatted for a bit. After he left I opened the door, took off my white pumps, and stretched out on the bed.

What happened?

When I first met Boris, he looked so appealing. But that first meeting took place in winter (a time of year when even strong odors are less pungent), the window was open, and he was seated across the wide table.

When Lena called me the next day to find out how it went, I didn't know what to say. I told her that I didn't think Boris was right for me. But there was no fooling Lena. She knew me too well. "I know you're disappointed," she said soothingly, "but don't give up. It takes time to find the right man." And then she repeated one of my favorite Russian expressions, the one she always says when she's trying to cheer me up: "*Budyet prazdnik i na tvoyei ulitse*. There will be a celebration on your street too."

The following morning I went to parliament to hear Yeltsin deliver his State of the Union address. There was only one seat left in the chamber: next to a male journalist. From a distance he looked presentable enough—he was wearing a suit—but when I sat down next to him, the smell of his unwashed body was overpowering. Getting up during such a speech would have been unthinkable. I was stuck there for the entire two hours.

Body odor, stubborn and unrelenting, was quite common in Russia. You smelled it everywhere: on the metro, in trolleybuses, shops, restaurants, the post office. Even in parliament (the politicians were no better than the journalists).

"As far as bathing goes, our men are an absolute nightmare," commented Svetlana, who was quite fastidious about her own appearance. "Summers are the worst. When it's hot and you're standing next to some guy on the trolleybus, it's enough to make you pass out." Certainly some women smelled too. As a rule, though, women tended to be more conscientious about bathing than men.

But free-market reforms have changed the way Russians, particularly men, think about personal hygiene. One of the cornerstones of Yeltsin's economic reform program was encouraging foreign investment. The influx of Western companies created new job opportunities and a sea change in grooming habits as people realized that in order to compete successfully for such jobs, they had to conform to Western standards of cleanliness. Coming to an interview with greasy hair and yesterday's shirt just wouldn't do. Since most of the lucrative new jobs went to men, the most observable change was in their hygiene and their appearance.

I had become so accustomed to garden-variety Russian men—the kind who didn't believe in covering up natural odors like bad breath and perspiration—that I was often taken aback by the sight of the dazzling free marketeers, who walked briskly through the streets in dapper suits, holding elegant leather briefcases. Hair slicked back with gel for that fashionable wet look, they sported sunglasses—designer, of course—and a newspaper, preferably *Commersant*, a sort of Russian *Wall Street Journal*, tucked under one arm.

A few years into the Yeltsin era, freshly shampooed heads were also glimpsed in the metro, and some men were alluringly scented with cologne. Hints of musk and sandalwood—instead of sweat—drifted through the cars and tickled your nose as you paused before the sliding doors to get out at your stop. Some men even started using deodorant and mouthwash.

(Before reforms began, there were sightings of clean men on the street and even in the musty, grimy confines of the metro, but they were fleeting and highly dubious, a little like those Elvis sightings in Tennessee shopping malls—everyone loved to listen to such stories, but no one quite believed them.)

But only a tiny minority was transformed by the new corporate ethics. By 1995, soap, shampoo, and toothpaste were widely available and relatively cheap. Many of those who clung to the old notions about grooming did so out of habit. Like various other Europeans, most Russians don't consider it necessary to bathe daily. Before the revolution more than 80 percent of the population lived in villages. In the late 1920s, when the country was in the throes of rapid industrialization, millions of villagers deserted their wooden *izbi* (peasant bungalows) for the lure of the city. Standards of cleanliness in villages, where there is no running water, are quite different from what they are in cities. People toil in the fields from dawn until nightfall and go to the local bathhouse whenever they can spare the time. Many city dwellers still behave like their ancestors, taking a bath perhaps once a week, or even less frequently.

It's probably relevant, too, that housing is still inadequate. For those who live in communal apartments, taking a bath every day is impracticable: in the morning and at night, as many as twenty people might be waiting to use the bathroom. One must be quick or someone will bang on the door and shout, "Hey, you, hurry up in there!"

Some people don't even have bathrooms. As a child Lena lived with her parents in barracks for six years before they were finally given an apartment by the state (the Soviet-era waiting list, which still exists, promised cheap housing after an average wait of ten to fifteen years). "You can't imagine what an ordeal it was," she told me. "There were fifteen rooms with one or two families crowded into each room. We all had to cook on a small kerosene stove in the hallway, which wasn't safe—it often caught fire—and we had no running water, no bathroom, only an outhouse." She was so desperate to escape that, at the age of twelve, she began writing letters to then-leader Nikita Khrushchev. (He never responded.)

But even those who have bathrooms face obstacles. The hot water is turned off for at least one month every summer, often without notice. You turn on the faucet one morning and it sounds like an old woman choking. Of course one can always take a cold shower, but Russians believe that doing so is harmful to the central nervous system. So, when the hot water is turned off, most people either forgo bathing altogether or heat up just enough water for a sponge bath. (Personally I heated eight huge pots of water so that I could take a *real* bath.)

Russians also worry about the supposed hazards of daily bathing, which have been proved by "science." One of my neighbors, a forty-year-old nurse, told me that the health risks associated with such frequent washing—greater susceptibility to colds, bronchitis, and even pneumonia—were well-documented and that she was shocked at my ignorance. "Don't they teach you *anything* in American schools?" she asked as she pulled a large tome from her shelf. Opening the book, which was written by a Russian doctor, she showed me a passage that instructed readers to bathe once every two weeks and to wash their hair once every three weeks ("... hair that is washed daily will lose its luster and may begin to fall out, eventually resulting in baldness," the author warned). Still shaking her head in disbelief, my neighbor handed me the book and advised me to read it carefully.

The idea that bathing can lead to illness is not unique to Russia. In *Too Loud a Solitude*, a novel by the Czech writer Bohumil Hrabal, the hero declares, "I don't like baths . . . because if I had a bath I'd be sure to come down with something. I have to go easy on the hygiene. . . . But sometimes, when a yearning for the Greek ideal of beauty comes over me, I'll wash one of my feet or maybe even my neck, then next week I'll wash the other foot and an arm, and whenever a major religious holiday is in the offing, I'll do my chest and both feet, but in that case I take an antihistamine in advance, because otherwise I'll have hay fever even if there's snow on the ground." When I first read *Too Loud a Solitude*, which was translated from Hrabal's Czech, I considered the title and thought: Well, of course he's alone. He doesn't bathe.

One starry summer evening a few weeks after my date with Boris, I was sitting at my computer when I suddenly smelled smoke in my apartment. Terrified, I dialed 01 and waited by the kitchen window. About a half an hour later the doorbell rang.

"Who is it?"

"Vladimir Andreyevich Chernyakov. I'm with the fire department."

I opened the door. Standing before me was one of those impossibly good-looking men you see in cologne ads, casually holding a black leather jacket over one broad shoulder. He was tall and muscular with swarthy skin and a seductive smile. His lips were moving. He was saying something about the fire. Some kids next door burning leaves . . . everything taken care of . . . nothing to worry about. I nodded, trying not to stare. As he spoke, he looked at me intently, and I thought I saw ardor kindling in his eyes, but when I closed the door I was sure that I must have imagined it.

A few minutes later the telephone rang. It was he. He said that he needed to verify my name and address for the fire department's records. I repeated both for him, spelling my name out in Cyrillic. Something was a little off kilter here: he sounded unusually friendly. Could there be another reason for his call? Don't be ridiculous, I told myself. He's just doing his job.

"What is your profession?" he asked.

"I'm a journalist."

"Really? Whom do you write for?"

I told him.

"What do you write about?"

"Do you need this for your records too?"

"No," he said liltingly. "I just want to get to know you better."

We agreed to have dinner at Russkoye Bistro, a trendy new restaurant, the following Friday evening.

The next day I mentioned my encounter with the handsome fireman to my Finnish friend, Päivi, who worked as an accountant at a Russian company. Like me—and all my foreign women friends in Moscow—Päivi had not had a presentable date in quite some time. She gaped at me and said, "Maybe *I* should call the fire department."

It seemed that my luck was finally turning. I was ironing the new black skirt I was planning to wear that Friday when the phone rang. It was Vladimir.

"I was just thinking about you," I said.

"I've been thinking about you too—quite a lot. I just wanted to let you know that our plans for tomorrow night might not work out. I have to go shopping with my wife. The kids need new winter coats. How about next Friday?"

I couldn't speak. A full minute must have passed. I could hear him breathing on the other end; he was waiting for an answer. Stammering, I said something about not being able to make it and ended the conversation as quickly as I could. After I hung up, I unplugged the iron and put my new skirt back in the closet.

"I'm not surprised," remarked Sandra, a world-weary marketing executive who always wore Givenchy suits and expensive perfume, when I told her. "All the clean ones are married."

Another American friend, who dated a Hungarian whose habits were not much better than those of most Russian men, offered this piece of advice: "You have to be drunk. You still smell it, but it's not as bad." Since I don't drink alcohol (I don't like the taste), that caveat wasn't very helpful.

I asked Svetlana how she dealt with the problem. "I'm luckier than most women," she said, settling down on the couch in her living room with a mug of tea. "Anatoly bathes regularly."

"But what if he didn't? How would you handle it?"

I told her about Boris, who still called occasionally. "It's such a shame," I said dejectedly. "He's great in so many other ways. What do you think I should do?"

Svetlana looked thoughtful. "Take him into the bathroom, hand him a towel and a bar of soap, and say, 'Please, be my guest.'"

"I can't do that. *You* could do that."

"You're a typical American—much too polite," she said mockingly, pouring me some more tea and adding two spoonfuls of sugar and a smidgen of milk (just the way I like it). "If you want your relationship to progress to the next stage, so to speak, you have to be honest with him. If you can't do that, then put a bag over his head, hold your nose, and try to enjoy yourself. You'll get used to it."

"I don't think so."

Maybe my standards were too exacting, I thought. After all, I grew up in the United States, where people deodorize every inch of themselves, not to mention pets, cars, rooms, refrigerators, carpets, toilets, garbage cans . . .

"You'll climb Mount Olympus to get clean," a British friend once teased, and I suppose it's true. No matter where I am, I always find a way. Stranded in a desolate village by the Black Sea, the name of which I don't even remember, I took refuge in the only shelter I could find: a wooden shack with a dirt floor, a filthy foam rubber mattress, and a rusty metal cupboard. Although it was past midnight, it must have been about 100 degrees. Inside the shack it was even hotter, since there were no windows, and my skin soon felt sticky and grimy. The next morning I discovered that there was no running water in the village. In fact, water had to be trucked in once a week. I found out (from one of the villagers) when the truck was coming and walked five miles to the outdoor shower stall where it was to deliver its precious cargo. I ended up with blisters on both feet, but it was worth it.

I once went out with an immaculate Austrian businessman named Rüdiger. We saw *The Terminator* dubbed into Russian—with one female voice reading all the characters' lines, even Arnold Schwarzenegger's. Afterward we went for a long walk in Sokolnikiy Park, and he offered to escort me home. By the time we got to my apartment, it was late and we were both hungry, so I invited him in for an impromptu dinner. As we sat in my kitchen eating pasta with little slices of ham and a small salad, he regaled me with dull stories of his misadventures in the business world, like the time he ordered a new computer from Germany. When it failed to arrive, he sent his secretary to the airport to investigate. She discovered that the computer had arrived all right, but the customs officer wanted Rüdiger's company to pay a fifteen-thousand-dollar duty. (The computer cost five thousand dollars.) "Zis vas ridiculous," he fumed.

I know it sounds strange, and I feel embarrassed just thinking about it, but I found myself feeling attracted to him. I couldn't understand it. And then it hit me: *he's clean.* It had been a long time since I had gone out with a man who was so well-scrubbed—three years, to be exact. As Rüdiger was hanging up his coat, he took out a small aerosol breath spray and discreetly sprayed a bit of the sweet-smelling potion into his mouth. After dinner he asked to use the bathroom. I could hear him spritzing again. I smiled to myself. Really, all this spritzing was a bit much. He outdid even me, a veteran spritzer. Still, it was better than the other extreme; at least he cared about how he smelled. When he came out his hair was freshly combed, and I caught the scent of his aftershave. . . . For a moment I looked at him longingly. But you're not really interested in him, I reminded myself. He's boring. And so I stood there, trying to think of a way to end the evening without offending him. I finally told him that I had to get up very early the next morning and that I really needed to get to sleep. "In that case," Rüdiger said, "I wish you a good night, and I shall call you next week." He gave me a peppermint-flavored kiss on the cheek and left. Later, the smell of aftershave and peppermint still in the air, I wondered if I had made a mistake.

When I told Tanya, a chain-smoking Canadian journalist, about this episode, she admitted, somewhat sheepishly, that lately she had felt attracted to Dima, a shady KGB-type who claimed to be a theology student. Tanya had known Dima for about a year and had often said that he was weird. I asked her why she was suddenly interested in him. (I had met Dima and agreed with her initial assessment completely.)

"He has some good points," she said evasively.

"Name *one*."

"Well, he . . ."

"Go on."

"Well, he doesn't stink."

Just as I suspected. Clearly, the situation was desperate: it was time to take action. Late one Saturday night Tanya, Päivi, Sandra, and I went to a splashy bar inside the Penta Hotel. They often played loud American disco music, which none of us liked, but the menu had all the familiar foods we craved. Sandra ordered a hamburger and a Tuborg beer, Päivi opted for shrimp scampi and a Diet Coke, and Tanya and I asked for Caesar salads and seltzer water. While we were waiting for the waitress to bring our food, I proposed a solution to our common problem: Why not start a social club for foreigners? We could put an advertisement in one of the city's English-language newspapers and split the cost.

Sandra and Päivi endorsed my plan enthusiastically. Tanya, who at twenty-three was the youngest in our little group (the rest of us were between twenty-five and twenty-eight), was reluctant. "I can't believe you guys are serious," she said, brushing a lock of her long auburn hair from her forehead. "I can't tell my mother this."

"Who says you have to tell your mother?" Päivi asked.

"She calls every week."

"So?"

"All right, let's figure out some of the basics," interjected Sandra. She took off her perfectly tailored black blazer, which was set off by a peach-colored blouse and a strand of pearls, and crossed her long, shapely legs. "What age group do we want to target?"

"Wait a minute," interrupted Päivi. "I just thought of something. How can we be sure they're not married?"

"We can't," I told her, "They can always lie. We'll just have to hope for the best."

"How do we know that they'll be any cleaner than the Russian men we've been meeting?" Tanya wanted to know. "My sister spent a semester in Paris last year, and she said that the men there smelled too. Maybe we should eliminate anyone who sounds French."

"I have some figures at work," Sandra said authoritatively. "According to our research, there are about seventeen thousand foreigners in this city. I don't think we have a breakdown by country of origin. I'll have to check. But a fairly high percentage must be American—just look at all the American companies that are here."

That was true, we all agreed.

"How are we going to weed out all the kooks?" asked Tanya, spearing a piece of cucumber with her fork.

"Maybe we should interview them," Sandra suggested.

"I don't think that's such a good idea," I said. "We'll scare them off. How would you like to be interviewed by a panel of men?"

"She's right," sighed Tanya. "It'll never work."

"Maybe I should do it alone then," Sandra said brightly. "I interview people in focus groups all the time."

"That's just the problem," I observed. "We don't want these guys to feel like they're a product that's about to be tested."

"I guess it could be a little awkward," she conceded.

"To all the clean, desirable men who are somewhere out there!" exclaimed Päivi.

We clinked glasses.

"I'll drink to that," said Sandra, tipping her head back and downing the rest of her beer.

The next morning I placed an advertisement in the *Moscow Tribune*: "Single foreigners aged 25–35 working/studying in Moscow wanted for get-togethers. Let's explore the city and get to know each other in the process. Call or fax brief letter to: 715-6939."

Unfortunately, the advertisement appeared in the "Personals" section (I had asked that it be placed under "Miscellaneous") directly underneath one that read, "Bisexual 36-year-old Italian man seeks companion of either sex for fun and adventure." During the next two weeks, my phone rang at all hours. Of the sixteen people who called, fifteen were men—and only one sounded normal.

One young man, who said that he was a professional samba dancer from Brazil, told me a long, convoluted tale about his brother's attempts to make a career for himself as a stripper ("but a tasteful one") in Russia. He said, somewhat obsequiously, that he loved Americans and wondered if I could help him get visas to the United States for himself and his brother—they had always wanted to see New York. Another man, a fisherman from Fiji, wanted to know if he should bring condoms and which kind did I prefer: lambskin or latex? After learning that I was of Ukrainian descent, a Ukrainian businessman, who insisted on speaking English (though he spoke it slowly and with great difficulty), said that fate had obviously brought us together and asked if I would meet him for coffee at the Slavjanskaya Hotel. A man with a heavy Middle-Eastern accent kept calling and repeating the same phrase: "I want you to come to my place." I hung up, but he persisted. Finally I stopped answering the phone.

As for the one man who seemed normal, an Indian who called himself Warren but said that his real name was Suresh, the last I heard of him, he had embezzled thirty thousand dollars from a British pharmaceutical company and absconded to Bombay. Not a smart move, I thought, since he was *from* Bombay (at least, that's what he told me) and that was probably the first place the police would look for him.

About a year later, Tanya, who never acted on her short-lived attraction to Dima, introduced me to an American journalist she met at a birthday party. "He's perfect for you," she told me excitedly. I thought so too. Until our third date. That's when I noticed that Sam's hair had slick patches here and there. I assumed that he used styling gel, but those oily spots turned out to be nature's handiwork. I was crestfallen when he told me that he showered once a week—and that he had no intention of changing his habits. "It's not like it's bad for your health," he said.

"But why?" I asked him over the telephone one evening. "Why only once a week?"

"I like dirt," Sam explained. It was a "gender thing," he told me. Women were much fussier about hygiene than men. "The problem isn't that I'm not clean enough," he said. "The problem is that you're too clean."

After I hung up I was so depressed that I almost called Dima. But *that* is another story.

Life is Cheap in Our Country

SPRING. THE SKY IS FLUSHED a soft, cotton-candy pink. Birds are twittering, and the sweet fragrance of lilacs fills the air. Maria, an American friend, and I are walking to the metro. We stop. In front of us is a traffic policeman in a long blue coat. He is standing in the middle of a six-lane intersection directing the oncoming cars with his white baton. Nothing unusual about that. But what is that on the ground? He is touching something with his foot, the way one does with an injured animal to see if it is still alive. We speculate that a dog has been hit by a car. But when we draw closer, we see that it is a man lying in a pool of blood. The man, who is perhaps forty or forty-five, appears to be unconscious. His body is still except for his arms and legs, which twitch spasmodically every few seconds. He is wearing faded blue jeans and a red-and-white checked shirt. His blond hair is matted with blood and clings to his sweaty forehead. The policeman kicks him in the ribs. "Come on, you," he sneers, "Get up!"

"We have to call an ambulance," I say to Maria. We try all three pay phones on the corner, but none of them work. "Let's go to Tanya's," Maria suggests. We run to our friend's apartment and ring the bell. Maria tells her about the man

while I dial 03, the emergency number of the state ambulance service. *Busy.* I spend the next half hour dialing, but I
can't get through. Exasperated, I slam the phone down.
"What are we going to do now?" We decide to call the
American Medical Center, which is staffed by both Russian
and American doctors. Today is Saturday, but perhaps they
have someone on duty. The phone rings. A young Russian
woman answers.

"What's going on?" Maria asks me in a whisper. "What
are they saying?"

"They want to know if he's a member of the center!" I
whisper back, cupping my hand over the telephone. "Look,"
I tell the woman at the other end, "we don't know him. We
have no idea if he's a member of your—"

Tanya takes the receiver from my hand. "For God's sake,
a man is dying. Do you understand what I'm saying?"

The woman repeats, rather stonily, that unless the man
is a member of the center there is nothing she can do. "Why
don't you call the state ambulance service?"

"We already tried that. The line's busy."

"I don't know what to tell you," the woman replies curtly
and hangs up.

Tanya puts the phone down. Her large blue eyes fill with
tears of helplessness and rage. The three of us look at one
another, silently wondering what to do next. "I'll call the
family I used to live with," Tanya says at last. "Maybe they'll
have some ideas."

She tells Masha, the mother of the family, about the man
and recounts our efforts to call an ambulance and what the
woman at the American Medical Center said. "That's the

way it is here," Masha tells her. "Life is cheap in our country."

Tanya hangs up and bursts into tears. "Now what?" she asks. Maria puts her hand on Tanya's shoulder. "It's okay," she says soothingly. "Think, who else can we call?"

Tanya phones a doctor she knows. He takes down the address and promises to meet Maria and me at the intersection. "I'll be in a blue Lada," he says. I check my watch: 6:28. Nearly an hour has elapsed since we saw the man. Maria and I run back to the intersection and wait.

Two hours later. The first stars are glittering. Cars zoom past the man, and the policeman waves his baton. Now and then he kicks the man in the face. "God damn you!" he shouts, staring down at him contemptuously. The man raises his right hand, which is covered with blood, as if he were trying to defend himself against the blows. For a moment his hand hangs in the air, as though someone were holding it there, then drops to the ground limply, the palm outstretched. The policeman is speaking into a walkie-talkie, but his voice is low and I can't hear what he is saying. It's 8:45. Where is the doctor? Could he have gotten lost? No, that's impossible. Tanya said that he lived nearby and knew this area well.

An ambulance arrives. A small white van with the words SKORAYA POMOSCH (literally, "quick help") written in red letters on the side. One jovial attendant checks the man's pulse. He says something to the other one, who laughs and pulls a white sheet over the man's face. They load him roughly into the back of the ambulance, as one might do with a pile of lumber. I notice a glimmer of gold, something shiny on the man's finger. I can't be sure—it's dark and there are no streetlights—but it looks like a wedding band. Most likely it *is* a wedding band. In Russia people tend to marry in their early twenties. It would be highly unusual for a man in his forties still to be single.

Life is cheap in our country. As the night air grows colder, the words keep flashing through my mind.

Maria and I take the metro home. I get off at Pushkin Square and walk to my apartment, a little dazed. I can't stop thinking about the man. Perhaps he had been on his way home from work and was struck by a car. But why did he attempt to cross a six-lane intersection? To get to the other side of such a busy street, pedestrians normally go through an underground tunnel. Maybe he was drunk (I had often seen drunks weaving through busy streets, especially on weekends, when the week's meager earnings are frequently spent on vodka). Whatever the circumstances surrounding his death, he was someone's son; his parents will surely miss him. His wife will be a widow. His children, if he had any, will be without a father. They will never know that the man spent the last few hours of his life being kicked by a traffic policeman who quite possibly hastened his death. They will never know how long he had lain there, in the middle of the street, or that he could perhaps have been saved. And I have no way of telling them.

The man's body will soon be inside a musty drawer in the nearest morgue. If there is no room, it will remain on a stretcher in the corridor for hours or even days.

His wife will probably begin by calling all his friends. When they tell her that they haven't seen her husband, she will sit by the telephone and wait for him to call, still believing that he is all right. By tomorrow morning, she will start phoning hospitals. No, they will tell her, there is no one registered under that name. Maybe you should check the morgues. Although she does not want to face the possibility that her husband might be dead, she picks up the phone again and begins dialing. But there are 10 million people in this city and God knows how many morgues. It will be virtually impossible to find him . . .

The man died in 1992. Four years later, in the spring of 1996, Tanya and I were walking past Byelorussky train station when a truck drove onto the sidewalk and headed straight toward me at full speed. Tanya pulled me out of the way by the sleeve of my sweater. We stood there, motionless, as the truck—which had come within inches of my body—roared past us, the driver completely oblivious to the fact that he had nearly hit me. Still numb with shock, we walked on in silence. Moments later another truck drove onto the sidewalk. This time the heavy metal door on the driver's side swung open as we were passing by—narrowly missing my head. The driver blithely reached out to close it and drove off.

In the winter of that same year, I was standing at a traffic light in front of my neighborhood grocery store, waiting to cross the street, when something hit me from behind and I suddenly felt myself being lifted off the ground. I realized with terror that I was on the trunk of a car and that we were headed toward one of the busiest intersections in Moscow. I jumped off before it began to pick up speed and landed in the snow. When I tried to stand up, jolts of pain coursed through my back and legs, although, as far as I could tell, nothing was broken. "Are you crazy?" I shouted at the driver.

"Didn't you see me when you were backing out? You could have killed me!" He scowled and looked away, as though he couldn't be bothered. His companion, a bleached blonde in a fur coat, stared at me with indifferent eyes as she munched on a cookie that she pulled out of a small, shiny bag she held in her hand. The driver cast me one last look of disgust before he drove away. As I made my way home, still trembling with rage, it began to hail, and I suddenly realized that in Russia my life was cheap too.

Later I wondered: Why was human life worth so little, and how was it possible for a society to live this way?

In a sense the question sounds naive. After all, the Communist regime slaughtered sixty million people. "We must kill more professors!" Lenin wrote in an urgent cable shortly after the Bolshevik coup in 1917. The idea that people are plentiful and, therefore, expendable, became deeply lodged in the national ethos.

It manifests itself in a thousand ways, this collective indifference to human life. Cars are not tested for safety—the idea has simply never occurred to anyone. Food and alcohol are not subjected to any controls either. People often get sick from poor-quality meat, vegetables, and dairy products and consider this normal. Contaminated alcohol is sold in kiosks. People drink it and die; no one is held accountable.

The Russian Health Ministry admits that half of the country's twenty-one thousand hospitals have no hot water, a quarter have no sewage, and several thousand have no water at all. Under such conditions infections are rampant, and many patients die.

Of course there is no number to call such as 911. There are three emergency telephone numbers: in addition to 03,

the number for the state ambulance service, one can dial 01
to reach the fire department, and 02 for the police. However, one usually gets a busy signal.

How can an emergency telephone line be busy?

It is well known that the operators often take the phones
off the hook so that they can relax and not be bothered with
emergencies. Sometimes the antiquated circuits are simply
overloaded.

Other public services are lacking. Somehow the authorities in Moscow never seem to get around to clearing the
snow. Every winter the streets, sidewalks, and the steps that
lead to metro stations become permanently iced, turning the
city into a gigantic skating rink. Every few feet you see someone—often a frail old *babushka*—slip and fall with a heavy
thud. I once fell with such force that I knocked a banana
vendor off his feet. I was in a hurry and didn't see him sitting in front of the metro, with his wares stacked on a small
table, until it was too late. Before either of us knew what
was happening, we were both prostrate and there were bananas everywhere (I tried to help him pick the bananas out
of the slush, but he shooed me away. "You've done enough,"
he muttered). When I took a shower that night, I noticed
that the area around the small of my back had a purple and
green bruise the size of a Frisbee. I couldn't sit or lie down
for three days without excruciating pain.

The evening news included a tally of how many people
had fallen and broken a limb that day (during one particularly harsh winter, it seemed to get higher with each broadcast). Yuri Luzhkov, the city's authoritarian mayor, dutifully
promised to bring out the snow plows whenever an interviewer asked him what he planned to do about the situa-

tion. But it was rare for anyone to ask, and of course nothing changed.

No wonder the life expectancy in Russia is lower than in any other developed country: fifty-eight for men and seventy-three for women. (In the United States, the life expectancy is seventy-two for men and seventy-nine for women.)

But the most astonishing fact is that deaths are now almost twice as common as births, although perhaps that is not so remarkable under a system in which everything seems designed to destroy the individual. What I find amazing is that people don't die sooner in a country where the government has traditionally spent the bulk of its resources on the accoutrements of war while skimping on things like medicine, agricultural production, consumer goods, and anything else that had nothing to do with rockets or missiles. During the Cold War roughly 85 percent of the national budget was devoted to defense spending. Even now, while the United States allocates more than 12 percent of its federal budget to health care and Britain spends 6 percent, Russia typically budgets slightly less than 1 percent—about the same as some of the poorest countries of Africa.

Under Communism, which was supposed to be a "higher form of social organization," the sole function of the individual was to serve the group, the collective, society: individualism became a crime. This was what the "glorious future" looked like—the world satirized in Yevgeny Zamiatin's book *We*, in which people wear identical uniforms and have state-designated numbers instead of names, I-330, D-503, O-90.

This collectivist mentality pervaded every institution from the schools to the agricultural system to the secret police.

Even the so-called helping professions were tainted by this philosophy. Doctors pledged, in the equivalent of the Hippocratic oath, "to work conscientiously toward the interests of society," not those of the patient (a convenient rationalization for locking up troublesome political dissidents in psychiatric hospitals). I can't help thinking that perhaps this value system had something to do with why the young doctor never came to the intersection to help the dying man. After all, what did it matter if one person—quite possibly a drunk, no less—died? As for me, I had become just another member of the faceless horde.

Politicians and newspapers in the West talk about the "collapse of Communism" and the ascendancy of democracy in the "new Russia." But Communism is not so easily banished. It lives on, inside people, long after power has changed hands and new flags have been raised. Certainly most Russians would never behave as the traffic policeman did. But too many people still treat one another with contempt, mistrust, and vicious cruelty. There is a word for this in Russian for which there is no English equivalent. People often speak of the *byezdushnost*, or "soullessness," wrought by the Communist period. The kindness and compassion that human beings feel toward one another under normal circumstances—if their souls have not been tampered with— was, in all too many cases, virtually obliterated.

It happened one sunny morning when people were strolling dreamily down the rose-strewn path to the "shining future." Somewhere along the way the clarion call of "the interests of society" resounded. The sound, which no one had ever heard before, was loud and thunderous and a little frightening at first. Young children hid behind their mothers, and animals scudded away to safety, as during a storm. But the Communists managed to convince everyone that it was the most beautiful sound that they had ever heard, and soon no one wanted to listen to anything else. Even music seemed dull by comparison. Nothing was more precious—not even the sound of a human voice. Husbands secretly hummed it to themselves while their wives were speaking to them over breakfast. Mothers preferred it to the sound of their children's laughter . . .

A kind of fantastically accelerated evolutionary process had occurred. Human warmth shrank into something like a vestigial organ, a bit like the appendix. A person could live and even thrive without it. The Communists (who saw themselves, to borrow Lenin's eerie phrase, as "engineers of human souls") decided to call this exquisite creature of the future, who would walk upright and learn to speak beautiful lies, "Soviet man."

The traffic policeman heard the clarion call of the Communists. He knew instinctively that he was supposed to protect "the interests of society." That is why his only concern was how to get the man's body out of the way. After all, one of the things the state is supposed to do is to keep traffic moving smoothly. How can it do that when there is a body lying in the middle of a six-lane intersection? Cars were honking, and people were beginning to get impatient. The road had to be cleared immediately. The policeman would have done no less had a tree fallen in the middle of the intersection.

Other servants of the state are also quite clear about where their allegiance lies. Consider, for a moment, what would happen if you went to a subway station in New York or London and tried to board a train without paying: you simply wouldn't be allowed to. In Moscow you would meet a much harsher fate: a pair of black metal arms would snatch you as you tried to pass. This can be shocking and frightening (not to mention painful), because the arms are carefully concealed. Like a thief in the night they reach out and grab you.

Those surreptitious hands seized a young woman one morning. The woman had placed a green plastic token in the slot but, as often happens, the token turned out to be defective. Somehow, she managed to get to the other side. But the *dezhurnaya*, whose job is to preserve law and order inside the metro, ran out of her glass booth and began berating her, accusing her of trying to cheat the state. They got into a shouting match, and the blue-uniformed matron punched the young woman in the face, knocking her to the ground. The woman lay unconscious, a small stream of blood oozing from her temple. The *dezhurnaya* looked down at her for a moment. She then marched calmly back to her post, apparently satisfied that she had done her duty. Someone eventually called the police. But when they came, they congratulated the smiling *dezhurnaya* for a job well done and didn't even bother to call an ambulance.

When Tanya told me that story, I recalled something one of President Boris Yeltsin's advisers said to me. Sergei Vitsin, who serves on the presidential clemency commission, which was created to reduce the growing number of death sentences by mitigating the severity of the punishment (the condemned are killed by a bullet to the back of the head), said that people were often outraged when he told them that such a commission existed. "But how can a criminal be granted clemency?" they asked him. Russia's judicial system is also based on the premise that the rights of the collective supersede those of the individual: you are guilty until proved innocent. Perhaps this is why few Russians express much pity for an innocent person who ends up in jail. After all, what is one life balanced against the safety of society? "Once someone is accused of a crime, the charge becomes immutable, like a stain," Vitsin told me. "Everyone automatically assumes that the person is guilty. He becomes a 'criminal' and nothing can change that." Perhaps the onlookers in the metro decided that the young woman must have been guilty because the *dezhurnaya* accused her of not paying. Maybe they thought she deserved what she got.

All this probably sounds incomprehensible, especially to anyone who has never lived in this part of the world. But how could it be otherwise? Those who were not ready to enter the Communist paradise were branded SHE (Socially Harmful Elements) or SDE (Socially Dangerous Elements). Such people were often sentenced to a labor camp or internal exile or both.

*   *   *

I met one of these torchbearers in Kiev, the capital of Ukraine. Semyon Gluzman, a psychiatrist, did the unthinkable: he refused to falsely diagnose political dissidents as mentally ill and in need of "treatment." And so he became a dissident himself. He spent seven years in labor camps and three more in exile.

The first thing I noticed about Gluzman when I stepped off the train in Kiev and saw him standing on the platform, in the soft glow of the morning sun, was the color of his skin. His face was as ashen as a tragic mask. But what I remember most about him was his eyes. There was a look of ineffable pain permanently etched there that made me think of a painting of the Virgin Mary I saw hanging on a bare white wall in a dingy communal apartment in Moscow. It was done in soft, melancholy hues of brown and gray, the large round eyes transfixed in a haunted expression. I remember thinking that it was the saddest face I had ever seen. I knew his story from newspaper accounts, but I didn't really understand the magnitude of what he had suffered until then. That look had probably been there when he was released into the arms of his family. After that it became permanent, like a scar: the indelible stamp of Communism. We had never met before, but I picked him out of the bustling crowd instantly, just as he had said I would. When I called him from Moscow, he offered to come to the station to meet me. "How will I know you?" I asked. "You will know me," he said simply.

Standing in the bright yellow sunshine, he greeted me warmly and offered to carry my small black valise. As we walked to my hotel, his mien was subdued, almost grave. He moved and spoke with great economy, as though he had suffered enough and didn't want to expend any more energy than he had to. Another thing I noticed: he never laughed. Whenever someone said something funny, the corners of his mouth would crinkle into two small arcs and he would smile a little. But even when his lips smiled, his eyes never did. (Tanya told me that she had seen that same shadow of a smile on the face of another former dissident, a doctor who had suffered especially brutal treatment in the camps.) Looking at him was like looking at a ghost, I thought, the ghost of a once-vibrant man. I imagined him as a red-cheeked young boy, kicking a dusty brown ball around the court-yard of his shabby apartment building with his friends, his small black eyes sparkling with the glow of youth, and later, as a young man, bright-eyed and ambitious, a little shy per-haps.

When I met Gluzman he had been a free man for eleven years. He had thought that freedom would never come. But one blue spring morning in 1982, they told him that he could go home. He was thirty-six years old. He had not been in-side his apartment in ten years. It must have looked strange at first.

I imagine him shaving on that first morning home. He is standing by the edge of the sink. After each stroke he runs the razor under the water to rinse it clean. When he is finished, he grabs a towel that is hanging over the bathtub and wipes the last traces of shaving cream from his face. He looks at himself in the mirror and that is when he sees it— the horror and the madness of the camps—staring back at him through his own eyes. At that moment he probably re-alized that he would never be able to get rid of that look, that it would always be there, a searing reminder of the past that the Communists did not want him to forget.

Don't ask him what they did to him there, he doesn't like to talk about that, so other journalists had warned me. But the details of his life "there" were not what interested me. I only wanted to know whether he had any regrets. Had he ever wished that he had just gone along?

A difficult question to answer. "I was naive," he told me as we walked down a crowded street in downtown Kiev.

Bright-colored little Ladas whizzed past us, spewing great clouds of dark gray exhaust. Gluzman coughed a little, as he often did. "I didn't understand then what Soviet power was," he said quietly. "It's okay to talk about these things now, but back then I went to prison and ruined my life. It was a cruel system. A person who wanted to work honestly had to pay for it by going to prison."

On the other hand, one of the great ironies of the Soviet system: life in jail meant a certain measure of freedom. "I said whatever I pleased to the KGB, right to their faces. It was wonderful because they couldn't do anything—I was already in jail." And he smiled a little.

Gluzman's story is tragic, and yet there are countless others like him who were sacrificed needlessly, senselessly, to the great scrap heap of "socialist progress."

I once called a repairman and asked him if he could fix my doorbell. He said that he was busy at the moment, but promised to call me back in a couple of days. A week went by, and I still hadn't heard from him, so I called again. He sounded jumpy. I asked him what was wrong. He said that he had tried to call me but hung up after he heard a "suspicious noise."

"When I heard that sound, I panicked."

"What sound?" I asked.

"A high-pitched squeaking noise."

I realized immediately what must have happened: my fax machine had probably gone off, as it sometimes did when the telephone rang. I tried to reassure him, but he was convinced that the KGB was tapping my telephone and that I was part of an elaborate plot to ensnare him. He refused to come to my apartment ("I know who you are and what you're trying to do!"), and I had to find someone else to fix my doorbell.

I later found out (from the friend who gave me his telephone number) that he had done time in the camps. I should have guessed. Like the look in Gluzman's eyes, the repairman's (understandable) paranoia will probably never go away. It has insinuated itself into his personality and has become a part of him.

When I told Lena about the repairman, she nodded as though this was a familiar story. "The worst of it is that we don't even need the state to terrorize us anymore," she said. "We've become even more adept than the KGB at keeping the fear alive within ourselves. For us it's normal to be We've become even more adept than the KGB at keeping the fear alive within ourselves. For us it's normal to be a little afraid all the time."

He's More of a Feminist than Most Women I Know

I KNEW THAT SOMETHING was horribly wrong the moment I heard Marina's voice on my answering machine that night. On the surface her words sounded ordinary enough: "It's Marina. Please call me back right away if you can." It was her tone that disturbed me. She sounded agitated. As I played the message again, a shiver of fear ran through me. Like most of my Russian friends, Marina feels awkward talking to a machine and always hangs up if I'm not home. She wouldn't have left a message unless it was an emergency. I sat down on my bed and dialed her number. She answered the telephone on the first ring. "*Alyo?*"

"*Privyet.*"

"Lori, thank God you're here. I was afraid that you might be away. I thought maybe you had gone to New York to visit your parents." She sounded as if she had been crying for a long time. Her voice, barely above a whisper, was redolent of pain.

"What is it? What's wrong? Are Valera and the kids okay?"

"Andrei is dead."

I don't know how long I sat there, holding the phone. "Did you hear what I said? Lori, are you there?"

Andrei was thirty-seven. He had just gotten married and his wife, Sasha, was expecting their first child. They had finally managed to save enough money to buy a car and a three-room apartment (they had been living with Sasha's parents). Andrei had founded his own research institute and was working on a book about the history of abortion in the former Soviet Union. It was supposed to come out in Russia and the United States. "Just a few more chapters to go," he had said. "I can't believe that it's really going to be published in America."

I thought of all this as I sat on the edge of my bed, holding the telephone, unable to speak. "How? When?" I finally managed to ask.

Marina told me that Andrei had taken a train to Vishniy Volochok, a small country village about two hundred miles from Moscow. Two days later—Easter Sunday—he was dead. Since he had gone there alone, no one knew exactly what happened. Only one thing was known for certain: the *dacha*, or summer cottage, he had so lovingly built with his own hands had burned to the ground.

How he died was still a mystery. According to one account he was inside the *dacha* when the fire broke out and either burned to death or died of smoke inhalation while trying to escape. In another version of this story, Andrei was out running an errand. When he returned, the little wooden house was ablaze. He tried to extinguish the flames with water from a nearby well and suffered a heart attack (this was plausible, given Andrei's history of heart problems). In this scenario two village women found him and called an ambulance, but he died en route to the only hospital in the area, which was many miles off.

That was it; that was all she could tell me, Marina said tearfully. We wouldn't know anything for sure until after the autopsy.

I suddenly recalled something Andrei had said to me. There was only one drawback to living in Vishniy Volochok: the area was so remote that there was only one antiquated telephone for the entire village. To place a call one first had to stand in a long line, then dial a series of codes that often didn't work. "If anything ever happened out there—if there was a fire or something—I would be out of luck," he had said. "There would be no way of getting help."

When I hung up the phone, I noticed that my hands were trembling. I sat on my bed for a long time, trying to comprehend what Marina had told me. I thought about the last time I had seen Andrei, just three months before. We were sitting in a café drinking espresso from tiny white cups. He pulled a letter out of his sport coat pocket and handed it to me. "Take a look at this," he said, his face aglow. The letter, which bore the logo of one of the biggest publishing houses in New York, said that his book was not commercial. The material was good, but the style just wasn't right. The letter went on to say that the book could be marketed to nonprofit organizations, which could use it for educational purposes.

"Not commercial." Most people would probably have been disappointed by those words. But Andrei was different. He didn't care about the money. He simply wanted people to understand how the former Soviet Union came to have the highest abortion rate in the world. "People must think that we're barbarians," he once said to me. "I wanted to tell the story that we've been hiding for so long." He also hoped that policy makers abroad might learn from his government's mistakes and was especially pleased by the last paragraph of the letter, which said that his book could be distributed to family-planning clinics in Africa and Latin America.

Trained as a doctor, Andrei had firsthand knowledge of the alarming number of abortions performed in his country: six for every birth (nine times more than in the United States). While still in medical school, he began digging in archives and talking to people to try to find out why abortion had become the leading method of birth control. After fourteen years of research—his obsession, he called it—he discovered that Health Ministry officials had deliberately thwarted the production of contraceptives because abortions had become so profitable (many doctors earned handsome fees for providing "extra" services, such as anesthesia). In a propaganda campaign designed to discredit birth control pills, the officials warned that oral contraceptives could cause cancer and even madness. In true centralized fashion, a report detailing these so-called side effects was distributed to hospitals and polyclinics across the Soviet Union. Doctors began encouraging women to have abortions, which came to be viewed as routine and even healthy. (No wonder many of the women he knew had had five, ten, or even fifteen abortions.)

Horrified by these facts, Andrei decided to dedicate his life to reducing the number of abortions by providing women with modern contraceptives and educating them about their use. He would focus primarily on Russia, which had the highest number of abortions among the former Soviet republics. (In 1998, 98.1 per 1,000 women of childbearing age had the procedure, compared to 20 per 1,000 in the United States and 10 per 1,000 in Canada.)

He didn't have any office space yet or money to pay for it. All he had was an antiquated computer, a fax machine, and enough enthusiasm to fill a soccer stadium. His goal was to train doctors—who often knew little about contraception themselves—to teach classes on the subject and to encourage women to bring their partners. He would also monitor women's health (many women become infertile or die from botched abortions even today), send reports on his findings to the press, and try to persuade more Western companies to donate condoms and other birth control devices. (The production of contraceptives is still extremely limited in the former Soviet Union, and those that are produced are of such poor quality that many polyclinics rely on scanty donations from Western companies.)

It was an ambitious plan, but Andrei was indefatigable. I remember all the red tape he had to go through to register his institute. Anyone who attempts such a feat must be armed with an organizational chart of whom to bribe and how much to give each person, Andrei quipped. The process took months, but somehow he got through it.

He had wanted to call his brainchild the Institute of Human Sexuality, but decided that would be too controversial in a country still caught in the puritanical strictures of the Soviet period. He was afraid that people would be put off by the word "sexuality" and wouldn't listen to what he had to say. So he decided to name it the Institute of International Family Research. In Russia, the word "family" often serves as a euphemism for anything connected with sexuality or birth. The phrase "family life," for instance, refers to a married couple's sex life.

Andrei was willing to do anything to get his message across. A shy, self-effacing man who spoke only halting English, he had learned to give press conferences and interviews to both the Russian and foreign media. Once, he told me proudly, he was even interviewed by the BBC—in English.

Just before he died he went to Cairo for an international conference on population control (abortion was, of course, among the topics discussed). When he came back, he gave a press conference on the disastrous state of Russian women's reproductive health. I had wanted to go but couldn't make it for some reason. I can't remember why. It wasn't until a few weeks later that we finally caught up with each other. We made plans to go to a museum, but somehow we never did. I suppose we were both busy. "Let's wait until you finish your book," I said. "You'll have more time then."

The day after Andrei's death, I went to a meeting of a new women's group called Feminist Alternative (I was working on a story about the Russian women's movement and wanted to interview a few of its leaders). At the end, the women, who ranged in age from about twenty-five to fifty-five, handed out the latest issue of *You and Us: the Women's Dialogue*, a feminist journal with contributions from women in Russia, Eastern Europe, and the United States.

Sitting in a crowded metro car on my way home, I opened it and was shocked to see a large photo of Andrei. His hair, which had turned blond under the Egyptian sun, was neatly combed, his beard a little fuller than I remembered. He was wearing a tweed jacket, a rumpled white shirt, and a red paisley tie, which he had loosened a little. This must have been taken during his last press conference, I thought. His gaze was intense, his right hand outstretched, as was his habit whenever he was trying to make a point. How strange it felt to be looking at that picture—he looked so young and vital. There was no mention of his death. I wondered why. Then I remembered that the journal was a quarterly; they had probably gone to press months earlier. I scanned the article. There it was: the verbatim text of that final press conference, the one I had missed. "In the ten minutes that I have been speaking, fifty-seven abortions were performed in our country," Andrei was quoted as saying. "In the next half hour that we will spend together, 172 abortions will be performed, and by the end of the day, if everything goes the way it has been going, you can be certain that at least one woman will die of abortion-related complications." Whenever Andrei talked about the harm done to women's health by abortion, his entire countenance, normally so reserved, changed. I imagined his eyes flashing with indignation, his voice rising with passion, as he addressed his audience.

The metro came to a grinding halt. I got out and walked the fifteen minutes it takes to get to my apartment from Kievskaya metro station. When I got home, I tucked the journal into a kitchen drawer I never look in.

The next few days were a haze of pain and insomnia. When I was awake, I clung to the idea that Andrei had escaped somehow, and that his body had been found intact. But at night I was tormented by images of a body blackened and charred beyond recognition. For some reason I saw him lying next to the little white fence that he had built himself, in which he had taken such pride (though it was unlikely that it would have survived the fire). Sometimes I saw his body

lying on a white table in a provincial morgue. His clear blue
eyes were open in a grotesque expression, and there were
maggots swarming around his parted lips. It was unbear-
ably hot and the air was filled with the stench of death. As I
desperately tried to find my way out, wrenching the handle
of one locked door after another, I saw other bodies, but
they were all covered with white sheets and I was grateful
that I could not see their faces . . .

I would wake up in the middle of the night, my heart
pounding loudly. In the morning I was always exhausted.
During one particularly restless night, I woke up screaming.
It was just after 2 A.M. Breathing hard, I tried to calm down,
to will myself back to sleep. But I could not have been more
awake. I lay there in the dark, listening to the silence and
staring at the play of shadows on the ceiling, created by the
moonlight; they looked like butterflies. An old grandfather
clock chimed, loud and clear, like the peal of church bells.
Three, four, five o'clock. Dawn was beginning to break; sunlight poured through the window, shining on my face. Knowing that I would never get back to sleep, I got out of bed and
wrote this letter to Maria, who lived in Moscow for a few
years and is now back in California:

Moscow, April 28, 1995
Dear Maria,

I am incapable of sleep during these dark days and
thought that I would write you a letter to comfort
myself. I still don't know the details of Andrei's death
or whether there will be a memorial service here in
Moscow. As for the funeral, Marina says we could

take the train to Vishniy Volochok, which, oddly enough, goes only in one direction. For the return trip, she says we would have to take the bus—and the one to Moscow runs only once a week. Of course there is nowhere to call to find out the schedule. The bus comes when it comes. I suggested taking a cab back to Moscow. Marina promised me that she would look into it.

I keep thinking of that line from the poem by Edna St. Vincent Millay, "Childhood is the kingdom where nobody dies." I guess my childhood lasted a lot longer than most people's—I never had to face the death of someone I cared about until now.

I know that it will upset me to see Andrei lying in a coffin, especially if he was badly burned, but I really want to say good-bye. Today I kept thinking about all the wonderful times we had. (God, it feels strange to be writing about him in the past tense.) I thought about all the museums we went to and the lively conversations we had, about Russian art and so many other things, and the time we went to Washington Square Park in Manhattan last summer.

We had been walking around for hours. The afternoon sun was hot, so we stopped into one of those little Korean grocery stores and bought orange juice and some bananas. As we sat on a bench, still warm from the sun's rays, enjoying our simple meal, a child roller-skated past us and fell. The girl, who was perhaps six, tried to get up, but, unaccustomed to the skates, slipped and fell again. She sat with her hands under her chin, staring at the pavement. When she looked up, her tiny face was crumpled in unhappiness.

"I can't do it," she said with all the seriousness of a six-year-old who thinks that she is the only one who has ever fallen down twice while trying to learn how to roller-skate.

"Yes, you can," Andrei said with a smile. His eyes were sparkling with kindness. The little girl caught the magic in his eyes and smiled back. She picked herself up and skated past us, waving to Andrei, her dark ponytail fluttering in the wind.

Andrei would have made a wonderful father, don't you think? Now Sasha will have to raise their unborn child alone.

Luckily the Russian Academy of Sciences, where Andrei worked for many years, has offered to help her pay for the funeral. I don't know how she would manage otherwise. Inflation (brought on by Yeltsin's market reforms) has put the cost of a funeral, even a modest one with a simple wooden coffin, beyond the reach of many families. People get into debt just to pay for a decent burial service. (And even if they are able to raise enough money to pay the whole sum up front, they still have to bribe the gravediggers with a case of vodka.)

Sasha and Andrei's parents have gone to Vishniy Volochok to sort everything out. What a nightmare this must be for them. The village morgue is so poor that it can't afford refrigeration. Since we're having

dn't stop crying. "Try to
gently.
pose I should go back to
ike it. I hope that you are

All my love,
Lori

t the soul must be nourished
d that it is customary to leave
able exactly forty days after a
ul begins its journey into the
e food out after a couple of
suggestion, I left two slices of
g, a dash of salt, and a small
red at the modest meal I had
meant something to Russians,
. By this time tomorrow, the
egg rancid. What good was a

spend a quiet moment alone
get the chance to say good-
Marina said that taking a cab
ould cost about one hundred
blem; we could have split the
a driver willing to travel such
trip). Why was everything so

g in a large hall listening to a
l speeches. They are a few of

an unusually warm spring, the body will decompose quickly. They'll have to bribe the local authorities to get permission to bury Andrei there.

You asked me about the funeral. Marina and I were hoping that it would be here in Moscow, but he told Sasha that he wanted to be buried by his *dacha*, so it's just as well. Andrei had the soul of a poet. He often spoke of the beauty of country life and would wake up early just to see the sun rise. He would stand by the window and watch the orange and violet rays spread across the sky. A few years ago he was living in a little house in Princeton, New Jersey (he was a visiting scholar at Princeton University). The paint was peeling, the pipes were old and rusty, and one wall had a hole the size of a basketball. But Andrei didn't seem to mind—or even to notice. He told me how much he loved to listen to the birds sing while he ate breakfast. Each morning, after he finished his juice and toast, he would open the kitchen window and leave a plate of breadcrumbs for the squirrels and sparrows.

In a country filled with brooding pessimists who accept early death as inevitable, Andrei was an optimist. I still wonder how he could have been so cheerful when so many of the circumstances of his life seemed so bleak. Money was always tight, his health was poor, and his living conditions were abysmal. Before he married he lived in a communal apartment with thirteen other people, all of them strangers. There was only one telephone, which each person was allowed to use for five minutes a day. If Andrei lingered a moment longer, a chorus of angry voices would shout: "Your time is up! Get off the phone!"

Andrei was one of the busiest people I ever met, but he always found time for me. He spent a whole day helping me get settled in my new apartment. After we finished moving everything, he pointed out the numerous safety violations to my landlord. I can still see him surveying every corner with the diligence of a building inspector.

"This," he said, pointing to an electrical outlet that had been hastily secured to the wall with masking tape, "is a fire hazard. Will you fix it please?"

"Who is *he*?" asked Yura, my new landlord, sourly.

"A friend," I said, smiling.

Like many Russians, Andrei also had a keen sense of the absurd. He could see the humor in any situation—even the attempted coup, or "armed rebellion," as the government preferred to call it, of October 1993. I was doing some freelance work for *Newsday* on the day the bloodshed began, and had to sleep at the bureau chief's apartment, along with the rest of the staff, because it was too dangerous to go home. In the morning, when the fighting had subsided a little, I went back to my apartment to grab a toothbrush and a change of clothes. I checked my answering machine and noticed that there were two messages. The first one made me smile. It was from you. Do you remember? You told me in a caring, yet firm voice not to be "the crazy investigative reporter."

her kind words, but I co
get some sleep," she said

It's nearly 6 A.M. I su
bed, although I don't feel
well. Good-bye for now.

Svetlana also told me tha
before it can leave the body, a
a simple meal on the kitchen
loved one's death (when the s
afterlife). "You can throw t
days," she said. Following he
black bread, a hard-boiled e
glass of vodka for Andrei. I s
prepared. Obviously this ritua
but it seemed senseless to m
bread would be rock hard, th
plate of rotten food?

How I wished that I coul
at Andrei's grave. I never di
bye. I didn't go to the funeral.
all the way back to Moscow
dollars. But that wasn't the pi
fare. The problem was findin;
a distance (seven hours roun
difficult in Russia?

Four months later: I am sittii
group of women give inform

Russia's first feminists. Some of them are friends of mine. We're here to celebrate the fifth anniversary of the Moscow Center for Gender Studies. A feminist think tank that does research on women's issues, it is the only organization of its kind in Russia. The speeches are extemporaneous and often rambling, filled with nostalgia, history, and humor. Mostly, the women talk about the early days, when the center was just a crazy idea. A small group of women desperately wanted to start their own research center, but none of them had any money. They applied to various grant foundations in the West (there are no such organizations in Russia), and to their surprise, were awarded fifty thousand dollars, enough money to start the center. The audience, mostly women, cheers as someone recounts the story.

Marina is here. She is wearing a blue chintz dress and white-plastic-framed, slightly lopsided glasses. Everyone laughs as she recalls how she, "an ignorant scholar," was made the center's "financial person" because no one else would take the job (it involves keeping track of which taxes the center is supposed to pay and doing the payroll, two duties I know Marina abhors). "They tricked me," she teases. "I thought I was being made the head researcher."

An American from the John D. and Catherine T. Macarthur Foundation is introduced as the next speaker. His name sounds familiar, but I can't quite place him—until he asks us to join him in a moment of silence for "a dear friend who did so much for Russia's women and was taken from us so early.

"Andrei was like a bright comet that shoots across the sky and then disappears in a flash. He was only thirty-seven years old when he died—"

"Andrei is dead?" I hear a woman in the row behind me ask in a shocked whisper. Yes, I think, Andrei is dead. And I feel the tears starting in the back of my eyes. I take a deep breath and try hard to keep myself from crying.

Anastasia, the director of the center, who is standing next to the man, translates his words into Russian. She speaks in a brisk monotone. But after a few minutes, she stops and looks down, unable to go on. "*Izvinitye*. Excuse me," she says in a barely audible voice. The tears are streaming down her cheeks. She stands there for a moment, weeping softly, then collects herself and continues translating.

I should have anticipated that eulogy. Andrei had received a grant from the Macarthur Foundation to help him start his research institute, and many of the women who were in the audience that night knew him. "He's more of a feminist than most women I know," my friend Tatiana, who was sitting in the front row, once said.

A Russian journalist wrote in a newspaper article that there was only one man in Russia who might be called a feminist: savvy television talk-show host Vladimir Posner, who has also appeared on U.S. television. It evolved into a kind of joke. It's not true, I would think, whenever I heard anyone say it. There is another, less famous one.

I never thought that I could feel such a sense of kinship with a Russian man. Early on in our friendship, Andrei asked me if I considered myself a feminist. I answered him honestly, bracing myself for the familiar look, that mixture of surprise and disgust that I had seen in so many men's eyes. What I saw instead was a quiet acceptance, a look that said, *That's fine with me.* On one occasion he asked me (sincerely, not mockingly) whether I would mind if he helped me with my coat. Not at all, I replied, but don't get carried away. "It's one thing," I explained, "to help me put on my coat or even to carry heavy luggage for me. But please don't offer to carry my grocery bag, as the custom seems to be here, if all I have in there is a box of tissues." At this he smiled. "That *is* silly, isn't it?"

I knew that Andrei was different from most Russian men the first time I met him. I was writing about abortion in Russia, and everyone I interviewed said, "You really must speak with Andrei Popov." So I did. At the end of our interview, which took place at the Russian Academy of Sciences, I thanked Andrei and shook his hand. In Russia, women never shake hands with men—it's considered too masculine. (Instead, they demurely hold out one hand, to be kissed.) I was well aware of this taboo and silently reproached myself for lapsing into my American ways. But Andrei behaved as though this was a perfectly normal situation—he smiled and clasped my hand firmly. Other Russian men had just stood there, holding my hand awkwardly and wondering what to do with it, as one might with a friend's pet iguana. Much later he told me, "I had the feeling that you didn't go for that hand-kissing business. To be honest, I've never felt comfortable with it myself. It seems kind of inappropriate. I mean, there you are, interviewing me, and I'm supposed to kiss your hand, like some prince at a ball." He took my hand and kissed it playfully. "Prince Popov . . . What do you think?"

"Not as romantic as Prince Oblonsky [a character in *Anna Karenina*], but not bad."

I was so relieved to find that I could be myself with him.

I'm sure that other men ridiculed him for his commitment to "women's issues," such as abortion and contraception. He never said this, but it must have been true. Yet he continued his work. That took courage. I always admired him for that.

Once, when we were walking through a spectacular exhibit of Rodin's marble sculptures, I asked him why he did what he did: "I know that you want to help people, but there are lots of ways to do that. Why focus on abortion and contraception?"

He thought for a moment. "I don't know. That's a Freudian question."

I never did find another museum partner. One evening, about two years after Andrei's death, I went to the Central House of Artists alone. It had been one of our favorite places, and as I walked through the exhibits, lined with nineteenth-century paintings, I thought of him.

I still remember the first time we went there as clearly as if it were happening now. I can see his face, as we stood by a wall that evening, admiring a painting. I can hear his voice, as if he were speaking to me now.

When Andrei and I went to museums, it was always in the evening because they were less crowded then. I was reluctant at first. I was used to going during the day. But Andrei persuaded me to give it a try, and I soon became an enthusiastic convert. Sometimes we were the only people in the museum. It was marvelous. We could spend as much time as we wanted at each exhibit—without having to endure all that pushing and shoving. (Russians tend to accept such appalling behavior, which occurs not only in museums, but also in trolleybuses, shops, and even at academic conferences.)

The only drawback was the constant, hovering presence of the *dezhurnaya*, the dour old woman posted inside each exhibit, whose primary function is to scold anyone who has the audacity to speak. "Stop talking this instant!" we heard one such matron snarl at two teenage girls standing in front of a Matisse. "Did you two come here to gab or to look at the paintings?" the stout old woman demanded. The girls, who blushed with embarrassment, stopped talking immediately. Such scenes made me cringe—I couldn't help wondering if I was next. How I envied Andrei. He had a way of charming even the surliest *dezhurnaya*. It was a special talent he had. Some people can place their heads inside a lion's mouth without getting bitten; others know how to tame a *dezhurnaya*.

It was about 7:30 in the evening, and it was so quiet inside the Museum of the Revolution that we could hear the echo of our own footsteps on the parquet floor. We stopped to look at a large map of what Solzhenitsyn called the "gulag archipelago" of the Soviet Union. Tiny red flags marked the places where concentration camps once stood. There were hundreds of them. I wondered when the camps had been closed and what had become of them. Had they been destroyed? Had any of them been converted to other uses? Into museums, perhaps?

"Let's ask the *dezhurnaya*," said Andrei.

The *dezhurnaya*? Surely he must be mad, I thought, glancing at the sullen woman sitting impassively on a chair in one corner. She looked like the kind of person who would view smiling as a weakness. She'll never answer any of our questions, I thought.

Moments later, Andrei returned with Iron Lady in tow. She introduced herself as Galina Aleksandrovna and proceeded to give us an expert lecture. She looked a little uneasy at first, but seeing Andrei's attentive gaze, became more animated. Her face, which had looked so stern a moment ago, began to soften. It was obvious that Galina Aleksandrovna hadn't done this in a long time. Yet she was not at all dour or unpleasant. She had simply forgotten how much nicer it was to smile and be polite. What a shame, I thought, that most people were afraid to ask a *dezhurnaya* anything.

Andrei also had a mischievous side. Sometimes he could not resist provoking the less congenial *dezhurniye* we encountered. A few weeks later we went to the Museum of the Revolution again. We wanted to see a large, moving diorama with life-size figures in a glass case dramatizing the chaos of the Revolution of 1905. But it was nearly eight o'clock, and the museum was closing in half an hour.

"Hurry up. I haven't got all day," said the officious *dezhurnaya*, reaching into her pocket and pulling out a large key. We followed her down a dark corridor and into a musty room. "Where are you from?" she asked Andrei. "Are you a Muscovite?"

"Yes, as a matter of fact I am."

"And the girl?" she asked, cocking her head a little in my direction. "Is she a Muscovite too?"

"The girl," said Andrei, "is from a lot farther away."

"Oh, really? Which city?" she asked, regarding me with curious eyes.

Andrei and I exchanged glances.

"Actually, the girl is American."

"And is all the degradation, poverty, and humiliation in our country interesting to watch?" she asked me, her voice suddenly hard and bitter.

She then turned off the lights so we could watch the display. A tape recorder played dramatic background music, complete with gunshots and shrill screams. A horse, whose head and neck moved, neighed. Cattle stampeded, the sound of their hooves growing steadily louder as a raging fire consumed everything in sight. The horse, she explained, had been prepared by a taxidermist.

"Are the people real too?" Andrei asked with a puckish grin.

She glared at both of us. "Hooligan," she said.

Andrei laughed gleefully, delighting in the *dezhurnaya*'s irritation. As for me, I was trying not to laugh, but I couldn't help myself. In a moment she'll throw us both out, I thought. She scowled at me, and I expected her to call me some name too, but she didn't. Because Andrei and the *dezhurnaya* were both Russian, she felt that she could take a more familiar tone with him, but I, as a foreigner, was off limits.

Andrei had a knack for imitating people. He used his whole body and all the muscles of his face. I could hardly control myself when, as we were leaving the museum, he mimicked the *dezhurnaya*'s expression. We were still laughing when we got to the metro.

The Train Has Already Left the Station

WHEN I FIRST ARRIVED in Moscow there were so few Americans living in Russia that I was something of a curiosity, so much so that a Soviet journalist brought me to the radio station where he worked—to be interviewed by one of his colleagues. "You don't mind, do you?" he asked genially. Before I could think of a tactful way to say "Forget it" in Russian, I was sitting in a small room with a microphone in front of me. A young woman with long blond hair and rectangular blue glasses came rushing in. Quickly she attached a microphone to her sweater. "We're on in five minutes!" she shouted to a man across the room. "My name is Yulia, by the way," she said to me, as she hurriedly scrawled a few notes. I looked at the portrait of Lenin on the wall. Next to it was a big red sign. In elegant gold script were the words *Radio Yunost*, "Youth Radio."

I fidgeted in my black leather chair, crossing and uncrossing my legs. I had been in Moscow for only three weeks. What if Yulia used some Russian word I didn't know? What if I flubbed the conjugation of a verb?

"Excuse me," I asked her timidly. "Is this going to be live?"

"Of course," she said cheerfully, "but don't worry. Just be yourself."

"Three, two, one!" yelled a sound technician in ear-phones. "You're on the air!"

After a few preliminary questions about New York City ("Are the skyscrapers really as tall as they look in the movies?" "Is it true that everyone owns a Mercedes?"), Yulia asked me how old I was, what university I had graduated from, what had brought me to Moscow, and what I had done for a living before coming to the Soviet Union. When I mentioned that I had worked as a journalist at a small news-paper in Binghamton, New York, my affable host pushed the big, old-fashioned microphone closer to my lips and asked, "So, how much did you earn?" There was a long, awkward pause. "I'm sure that our listeners are curious," she prompted. Not wanting to embarrass Yulia, I reluctantly told her—and six million listeners—that my *zarplata* had been sixteen thousand dollars a year. I did not tell her that I often wrote about cats trapped in trees and cows that had been tipped over by bored and rowdy teenagers.

As I became more familiar with Russian culture, I realized that everyone earned only a token *zarplata*, so there was no need for secrecy. I noticed that the salary question was one of the staples of small talk, along with this popular conversation opener, "So, are you married?" Russians talk about marital status with the same ease with which Americans discuss the weather and sports. Although I never quite got used to telling strangers how much money I made, I always found this second question much more irritating. I was struck by the pity in people's eyes whenever I mentioned that I was single. Even then, at twenty-five, I was a pariah, someone whom fate had dealt a cruel hand. By the time I turned thirty, the pesky question dogged me wherever I went.

Cabdrivers, prospective landlords, and even salesclerks all wanted to know whether I was married. The query was posed so often that had someone been following me around with a notebook in an attempt to learn the Russian language, he would surely have supposed that the words, "*Vy zamuzhem?*" must be a form of greeting.

Some people couched their curiosity in euphemism. "Do you have a family?" they asked innocently. Not knowing the nuances of the question, I assumed that they wanted to know whether my parents were still alive and whether I had any siblings, so I always said yes. After I learned what my interlocutors really meant, I confess that I began willfully deceiving them—hanging noodles on their ears, as Russians say—to avoid the intrusive questions that inevitably followed. ("*Why* aren't you married?" "Are you a lesbian?" "Are you one of those man-hating feminists?") If I was feeling particularly adventurous, I even invented children. I did not do this purely for my own amusement. Once you say that you're married, the follow-up question is, "Do you have children yet?" I always said that I had two darling *detishki*, a boy and a girl.

One of the drawbacks of lying is that you must remember what lies you have told whom. I have a poor memory, but I figured that in a city of ten million, the chances of running into the people I had duped were infinitesimal. As luck would have it, I beat the odds.

It was 1:45 in the afternoon and I had just fifteen minutes to get to the bank before it closed, so I hailed a cab.

"Well, hello there!" said the driver. "Good to see you again. How have you been?"

I stared at him. Do I know this man?

"I picked you up in this same spot a few months ago," he said, referring to the curb in front of my building. "We had a very nice conversation about your family. How is your husband these days? And what about little Katya? You have a son, too, as I recall. Wait, don't tell me his name—Igor, right?"

He's obviously mistaken me for someone else, I thought. And then it all came back to me.

"Oh, they're just fine," I said, recovering my composure. "Thank you for asking."

"Have you gone back to work yet?"

"No, I'm going to stay home for a few more years. My husband says it's better for the children."

Such duplicity made me feel like a secret agent. Fortunately some of the Russians I met knew that people in the West tended to marry later. If I admitted that I was single, as I did if I thought that a new acquaintance might develop into a friendship, I was often dismissed as merely another eccentric foreigner and spared the standard lecture.

Russian women cannot escape the disapproving glances and questions quite so easily. Take my friend Yelizaveta, for example. It is a Thursday evening and she and I are sitting at my kitchen table. Yelizaveta, an actress, has just come from Moscow State University, where she is studying to be a teacher because in the current economic climate, not many movies are being made. (Many cinemas have closed; those that remain feature mostly action-adventure flicks imported from the West.) It's cold outside, and she is still numb from the fifteen-minute walk from the metro, so I give her one of my sweaters to put over her shoulders. As I cut some bread and put the kettle on for tea, she speaks with bitterness about her *roman* with a callous young actor, which ended recently. I have heard this story before, but tonight I hear something else in her voice—fear.

"Look at me," she says. "I'm thirty-one, and I'm still not married. I'll die an old maid."

"You're a young woman," I tell her. "You have so much to look forward to."

"Like what?" she says, stifling a sob. "Don't you realize that time is flying? In a few years no one will want me!" She breaks down and cries.

I remind Yelizaveta, whose large blue eyes and small, round face still have a girlish innocence, of how many times she has been mistaken for an undergraduate at the university.

"Yes, everyone is always telling me that I look so young. I don't know if they're telling me the truth or if they're just flattering me. But no matter how young I look, it doesn't change how old I am."

I knew many Russian women who, like Yelizaveta, felt that they were failures because they were single. In Russia, both men and women try to marry as soon as possible. But the desirability of marriage is not fueled by a fervid longing to find one's "other half," as it is in American culture. In Russian eyes marriage is not a lifelong commitment. It is a rite of passage, a marker on the road to adulthood, much the way buying one's first car is in the United States. As Svetlana, who is forty-two and has been divorced for ten years, says, what's important is not *staying* married, but *having been* married. "Marriage is a necessary evil," says another friend, who is now seventy and was widowed at fifty-five. Those who have never been married are viewed as pathetic immature people who never fully graduated into adulthood because they missed out on a crucial stage in their social development.

Few can withstand the enormous pressure from friends, relatives, and even neighbors. Most actively seek out a mate during the college years just to avoid the stigma of being single. Women are, of course, especially vulnerable to such stigmatization. Many get married at seventeen or eighteen. Those who are over twenty-five and still single are often ridiculed.

But even if they are not mocked openly, unmarried women often feel their society's disapproval in other, more subtle ways. Working the late shift at TASS one evening, I took a break with Lyudmila, who was thirty-five. We were sitting on blue plastic chairs in the cafeteria, drinking strong coffee, and Lyudmila, who knew that I was flying to New York in a few days to attend a friend's wedding, asked if there was "anyone special" waiting for me back home. No, there was no one, I told her.

"That's a pity," she said.

"Why?" I asked.

"Because you have to get married. I don't know how it is in America, but here, married women are treated with more respect, especially at work." In fact, under the Soviet system, single women were considered "morally unstable" and their careers often suffered. "People try not to say anything, but I feel it all the same," she said with a tinge of sadness. "I know that they talk about me. They wonder what's wrong with me. I try not to dwell on . . . my situation, but sometimes I think that maybe there is something wrong with me. If a woman is single, it means that no one cares about her."

When Lyudmila first introduced me to her friend Anya, a swanky nightclub singer who had started her own record company, Anya told me that she was living with "a boring businessman" with whom she had "absolutely nothing in common." She added, quite casually, that he despised her family and would not let her see them. "He won't even let me talk to my mother on the telephone," she complained. On top of all that, Yegor had many clients in England and the United States, yet he refused to learn English. "I wish that he would learn at least enough to get by," Anya said wearily, "but he says that he doesn't have time to take classes. So, I have to do everything for him. Frankly, I'm getting sick of it." I was shocked when she referred to him as her "fiancé."

As Anya and I became better acquainted, I noticed that Yegor criticized her constantly and flew into fits of rage. She often called me in tears, late at night, after he was asleep. But she was reluctant to leave him. This went on for about a year.

We went to Gorky Park once, just the two of us. It was warm, so we took off our jackets and sat down by the lake. Wild ducks fluttered, and the midday sun gave the water a silvery sheen.

"Why do you stay?" I asked her.

"How can I explain it? It's like"—she paused for a moment—"like having an old suitcase. It's all scuffed up, the zipper is always getting stuck, and the handles are all rusty. You know you should throw it away, but you just can't bear to part with it because you've had it for so long. Well, that's how I feel about Yegor. Do you understand?"

I did, but I still thought that she should end the relationship, and I told her so. She looked away, staring at the sunspangled lake in silence.

After that Anya often referred to Yegor as her *chemodanchik*, her "little suitcase." She would laugh, and for a brief moment, the sadness would fade from her eyes.

A couple of weeks later, we were sitting in Anya's kitchen, sipping tea and talking about her wedding, which was just a few months away. It was almost eleven o'clock in the evening, but the sun had just disappeared behind a birch tree and the sky was a soft lilac; a warm June breeze stole through the window. Anya took a jar of raspberry *vareniye*, homemade preserves, out of the refrigerator and put it on the table, which was covered with a red-and-white checked tablecloth. We stirred a few spoonfuls into our tea.

"The marriage won't last more than a year or two," she said matter-of-factly.

"Well, if that's the way you feel," I said, "don't you think you should call it off?"

"No, I'm going to go through with it," she said with grim determination. "I've dilly-dallied long enough. I'm twenty-six already."

Time passed, and Yegor's abusive behavior continued. One midsummer morning, while he was out jogging, Anya called me. "I've had enough," she said. When he came back, she handed him the large, oval-shaped diamond engagement ring that he had given her the year before and asked him to move out. He cried, something she had never seen him do.

A little dazed and on the verge of tears herself, Anya sat down in the living room, wondering what she would do now. Her company had not yet become profitable, and Yegor had always insisted that she turn what little she did manage to earn over to him. She had no money of her own. But she did have one valuable asset: the luxurious apartment that she and Yegor had shared (it had been bequeathed to her by her grandfather, a career diplomat and loyal Communist, who was given the apartment by Soviet authorities). It occurred to her that she could rent it out. And she did—for $2,400 a month—about twenty-five times the average monthly salary. (She moved into a smaller but spacious place, which she furnished with beautiful, imported furniture.)

Anya is now a rich woman. Between the rent she collects each month and her new job as a travel agent, she earns $32,400—considerably more than most First Deputy Prime Ministers, whose annual salary is about $12,000. She can afford to travel (so far she has been to Brazil, Portugal, Switzerland, and Italy) and is even able to support her ailing mother and grandmother.

But she admitted to me recently that she sometimes wonders whether she made the right decision. At her age—she's now twenty-eight—Anya feels that she should have children. Which brings us to the second part of the equation. According to the Soviet constitution, which wasn't abolished until 1993, women entered into a tacit social contract with the state. In exchange for all the cradle-to-grave benefits the government provided, women were expected to serve the state as workers and mothers (producers of more workers). Having children became a civic duty.

Echoes of this dictum, which left an indelible mark on the female psyche, can still be heard today. Women are pressured by their families and even by doctors to have children as early as possible. Anya told me that her gynecologist has for years been urging her to have children "before it's too late." Svetlana, who had her son, Kirill, at twenty-three, was told by her obstetrician that she was "too old" to be having her first child. "What can I tell you?" she said, seeing the look of disbelief on my face. "The doctors in this country are idiots." Thirty-somethings are considered long past their childbearing years, which makes sense if one considers the fact that the average Russian woman is already a grandmother by the time she reaches her forties.

I was also pressured to have children, sometimes by people I hardly knew. *How do you expect me to do that*, I wanted to ask them, *when most of the men here think that bathing is something they ought to do only on special occasions?*

While spending yet another Saturday night watching one of those heavy-handed Soviet-era war movies (the only kind on then), I called my married friend Marina. She listened patiently as I told her how frustrated I felt. "I'm young and single, and I can't date," I complained.

Marina, who always knew how to make me smile when I was feeling down, said, "I have an idea. Why don't we build a special camp for men to teach them better grooming habits? We could put up signs: WOMEN OF RUSSIA, SEND US YOUR MEN!"

"Well, the birthrate would go up," I said.

"Yes, exactly," she giggled. "We could get the government to donate soap and shampoo. . . . Seriously, though, if you *do* find someone presentable—and if you look hard enough, you will—you really should get pregnant. You're twenty-seven. What are you waiting for? If a woman doesn't find anyone by a certain age, she should just have a baby on her own."

Several other well-intentioned friends gave me the same advice. I tried to explain that I didn't want children just then; I wanted to get married first. When I saw the bewilderment in their eyes, I realized that in Russia, whether a woman wants to become a mother is irrelevant. "Women who don't have children are selfish," the popular saying goes.

I saw the unfortunate consequences of such thinking when I flew to Syktyfkar, a smoggy, heavily industrialized city in the northern republic of Komi, in 1993. I was to interview Yekaterina Pavlovna Yarodkina, a woman doctor with no political experience who had decided to run in that year's parliamentary elections. As it turned out, Yarodkina, who was the head of the local hospital's cardiac unit, had little time to spare, and I found myself spending many hours with her campaign manager, a forty-four-year-old philosophy professor named Valentina.

Since Valentina (who bore an uncanny resemblance to Gloria Steinem) didn't know the first thing about the candidate whose campaign she was managing, including her hometown or even her age, we chatted amiably about a variety of other topics. (To be fair, Russia had for decades been a one-party state, where candidates ran unopposed and were "elected" by the majority without having to campaign, so no one knew exactly what a campaign manager was supposed to do. I suspected that Yarodkina thought she would make a better impression with the Western press if she had one.) She asked if I was married and whether I had any children. "I've never been married myself," she told me. "I simply couldn't find anyone who was cultivated enough for my taste. So, I had a child by myself. I had her very late in life—I was thirty-four. But better late than never, right?"

The door to Valentina's office was open, and, as we were speaking, her ten-year-old daughter ran into the room. "Well, look who's here!" Valentina exclaimed, smiling broadly. The little girl, who was still in her school uniform, a brown dress and a freshly starched white pinafore, sat on her mother's lap and linked her arms around her neck. Valentina hugged her and asked her whether she had started her homework. The child shook her head. "No? Well, we'll do it together." Stroking the girl's hair, she gently explained that she wouldn't be home until 7:30 and that she would have to heat up her own dinner, which was in the refrigerator.

Patient and loving as Valentina appeared, I had the strange feeling that she didn't really want this child. Her tone, her words—even her smiles—seemed forced. The whole scene looked staged, and maybe it was.

Valentina's boss was a candidate for the Women of Russia Party, which billed itself as a gentler, more compassionate alternative to the other, male-dominated parties. Campaign commercials portrayed these female candidates not as hard-nosed politicians, but as devoted wives and mothers, often showing them with their husbands and children. Women of Russia was founded, so the party's literature claimed, to promote the interests of women and children. It would not do, I thought, to allow a journalist to see a campaign manager behaving unkindly to her own child. But what did I know of this woman or her relationship with her daughter? After all, I had seen only one brief interaction. Maybe she was just overworked. Being a single mother and run-

ning a political campaign couldn't be easy. I was still absorbed in these thoughts when Valentina took the child's
hand and led her to the door. "Now, Natashenka," she said
sweetly, using the diminutive form of the girl's name, "I've
told you not to come to my office. Please don't do it again.
You know that Mama doesn't have time for you when she's
working." Natasha, who looked a bit chastened, apologized,
then left, blowing her mother a kiss. As soon as the child
was gone, Valentina's demeanor changed. Her voice took
on a bitter edge, her face a weary aspect. "Children don't
always fit into one's life," she said, no longer smiling. "But
what can I do? A woman can't escape nature. We're doomed
to have children whether we like it or not."

In Russia female-headed households such as Valentina's
have a long, venerable history. Millions of Soviet men were
killed during World War II, leaving their young wives to
raise their children alone. These women became symbols of
courage and changed popular notions about the family. Today, decades after the war ended, many Russian women are
choosing to have children on their own. Such women are
viewed with admiration. But how many of them are happy?
After I left Valentina's office that day, I wondered whether
she would have felt more fulfilled if she had remained child-
less. Quite possibly, I thought—until I spoke with Galina, a
member of the State Duma, the lower house of parliament.

I was doing a story on a new law that women's groups
feared might lead to a ban on abortion, and I had phoned
Galina, who was a lawyer, to find out more about it. Many
Russian politicians hid behind a coterie of aides, who shielded
them from anyone who might ask uncomfortable questions
(a holdover from the Soviet era when they were all-power-

ful members of the Communist Party and not accountable to anyone, least of all nettlesome journalists, for their actions). But Galina, one of the few Russian women I knew who dared to call herself a *feministka*, was always friendly and accessible. Whenever I ran into her in the ornate, red-carpeted halls of the Duma, she smiled and often stopped to chat. When I saw her at a party once, she embraced me vigorously and kissed my cheek three times. She even gave me her home telephone number, in case I ever needed to reach her in the evening. That morning Galina faxed me a copy of the law and invited me to stop by her office so that we could discuss it in person. I made an appointment for the following afternoon.

When I arrived, Galina asked her secretary to make us some tea. The secretary, whose hair was lavender—the shade favored by many elderly Russian women—came in with a large tray laden with butter cookies and a small cornflower-blue teapot, which she placed on the coffee table in front of us. Bending her purple head, she poured us each a cup of tea, then padded quietly out of the room, closing the door behind her. Galina spoke passionately about the need to amend the law, which mentioned a child's "right to life." As we talked about abortion, the conversation took a personal turn, as it often does between women. Galina, who was in her late thirties, confided that she had always wanted to have a child. She told me that the other women in her apartment complex, all of whom had children, shunned her. "People imply that you're not a real woman, that you're *defective*. Sometimes I feel like a man in a skirt."

She stared into her teacup. "I did try to get pregnant; but nothing ever came of it. I guess I just can't conceive."

"Not necessarily," I said. "Have you and your husband gone to a doctor?"

"No, I was always too embarrassed, and Yuri would never admit that he might be impotent. You know how our men are."

"Maybe the two of you can go together. Why not? It's not too late. You can still have a child."

"You don't understand. It's all over for me. The train has already left the station."

Galina explained that it would be humiliating to be pregnant at her age, the equivalent of a sixty-year-old in the United States conceiving through some extraordinary means.

Although the drive to get married and especially to have children—to catch the train before it leaves the station—is the keynote in most women's lives, many seem to regret their decision.

Marina (the woman who jokingly suggested building a personal-grooming camp for Russian men) is an ardent feminist married to a mathematician who openly disparages women. Over dinner one evening at my apartment, I asked her how she could live with a man who had such a different perspective. Marina acknowledged that her husband felt threatened by her work—she was a sociologist at the Center for Gender Studies—and by her colleagues, whom she proudly referred to as "the feminist elite in this country."

"Yes, Valera is patriarchal," she said, "but so was I when we first met. Anyway, there are some things about him that suit me. He's a scholar, like me; he doesn't drink much, just a little wine once in a while; *and* he's a good provider. He has always brought home enough money, which is more than I can say about a lot of other husbands I know. He is also civilized enough not to try to forbid me from doing the kind of work I enjoy."

But I couldn't help noticing that Valera didn't take much interest in their two children. I dropped by one Saturday evening to help Valera translate a letter into English, and we were sitting on a divan in the kitchen when their son, Ilyukha, came in to grab a chocolate chip cookie. "He's gotten so tall since the last time I saw him," I remarked. "How old is he now?"

Valera furrowed his brow. "I'm not sure. I would have to check with Marina." I was amazed.

Later that evening, I mentioned this episode to Marina, who had just put their five-year-old daughter, Ksenya, to bed. "No," she said ruefully, "he wouldn't know things like that."

Marina is usually full of laughter. But when Valera walks into the room, her eyes grow cold and the muscles in her face become taut. They speak to each other as little as possible. Mealtimes are especially tense. Instead of asking Marina to pass the *pirozhki*, Valera will get up and fetch the dish himself.

When I asked Marina if their relationship had always been like this, she told me that Valera used to bring her flowers and candy in the exuberantly romantic days of their courtship. "He really knew how to treat a woman," she said wistfully. But the niceties stopped soon after the wedding. Nowadays Valera is likely to forget his wife's birthday and seldom remembers their anniversary. After dinner he buries himself in academic journals, while Marina takes care of their children and does all the household chores. "The only thing that he does is take out the garbage," she says, "and I have to remind him five times before he does *that*." Mostly, she is too busy—and too tired—to argue, but now and then, her resentment rises to the surface and leads to an explosive argument after the children are asleep.

I was reminded of Marina's situation one brisk winter afternoon when Lyudmila and I were taking a walk around Moscow. We passed a church that had blue and white onion domes sprinkled with little gilt stars. It must have been below zero, and we stopped inside to warm ourselves. The church was empty except for a few *babushki*, who were kneeling on the stone floor and praying fervently. There was no music and there were no flowers, so we were surprised to see a bride and groom walk through the door.

The bride was very young, perhaps nineteen or twenty. Her dark hair was long and straight and her face, which was completely bare of makeup, was as pale as dawn. Her plain white dress, which looked as if she had sewed it herself, was too big and slightly crooked at the hem. It had no flourishes of any kind, not a single ruffle or hint of lace. The groom, who looked about twenty-two, wore a cheap navy blue suit. They stood several feet apart from one another, each holding a slim yellow candle. Their youthful faces, which should have been filled with joy, were sullen. There were no furtive glances, no shy, excited smiles. In fact, they did not look at each other at all. I wondered if the bride was pregnant and had been pressured into this by her parents. The old priest, who had his back to the couple the entire time, mumbled throughout the ceremony, as though he were talking to himself. He did not mention the couple by name.

I surveyed the cavernous church. Why had no one come? Didn't these two have any relatives or friends? (The *babushki* were clearly strangers.) As we were leaving, Lyudmila asked me what I had thought of the ceremony.

"They looked as if they were about to face a firing squad," I observed.

"They didn't look very happy, did they? I've been to so many weddings," she added with a shrug, "I'm used to it, I suppose."

I marveled at her complacent attitude. I couldn't help but wonder why the bride hadn't put on any makeup and why she hadn't styled her limp hair. But most of all, I wondered how she could have worn that dress, why she hadn't made any effort to make it look pretty. Perhaps, I thought, she hadn't had time. Perhaps she had been in a rush to board the train before it pulled out of the station.

A Coup to Remember

I HAD JUST RETURNED from a brief vacation in New York. The flight had been long and uncomfortable, and by the time I got back to my apartment on the Highway of the Enthusiasts, I was so exhausted that I went straight to bed. It must have been about two o'clock in the morning when the telephone rang. Dimly I heard a woman's voice on the answering machine—something about Parliament—but I was too sleepy to pay much attention. When I woke up, at 7:30, I remembered that someone had called in the middle of the night and got up to check my answering machine. "Hi, it's me." It was Sonia. "I just wanted to make sure that you know what happened. Yeltsin dissolved Parliament. I'm sure I'll see you soon. Bye."

Having been away for almost two weeks, I was a bit jet-lagged. I made myself some coffee and turned on the radio.

"Yesterday evening President Boris Yeltsin signed a decree ordering Parliament to disband. The president said that the 'irreconcilable opposition' of the legislature to his policies had made it impossible for him to govern and that new legislative elections would be held in three months."

The announcer went on to report that Parliament (which was dominated by hotheaded Communists) had voted to impeach Yeltsin and had named Vice President Aleksandr Rutskoi—a headstrong general and Yeltsin's archnemesis—acting president. Although Yeltsin had ordered the legislators to leave the White House, as Russians called their parliament building, a number of hard-liners had refused and spent the night building barricades from scraps of metal and blocks of concrete.

My first thought was: I've been back less than twenty-four hours, and already there's a crisis. In the two years that I had been living in Russia, the ruble had crashed several times; members of the cabinet had been fired, re-hired a few months later, then fired again; and Parliament had tried to impeach Yeltsin so many times that Yeltsin himself had probably lost count. Would Russia ever be a stable democracy?

I called the local bureau of *Newsday*, one of the papers I freelanced for. Ken, the bureau chief, answered the phone. "You came back just in time," he said. "Can you be here in an hour? I have no idea how long this assignment will last, maybe one day, maybe three months, but I need you from now until this thing is over."

When I arrived, Ken's wife, Susan, who worked at the bureau as a correspondent, was in her office, reading the latest news reports. Like me, she had seen it all and wasn't that concerned.

"Anything exciting?" I asked as I hung up my jacket.

"Not really," she murmured, without looking up.

Sonia, who was sitting in front of a computer, translating a newspaper article from Russian into English, turned around.

"Hey, welcome back to Moscow! Sorry I called so late last night. I wasn't sure if you'd heard. What time did you get in?"

"Around ten."

"How was the flight?"

"Terrible. I took Aeroflot [the former Soviet airline]. Thirteen hours, and all they gave us was one scrawny chicken leg, a cup of tea, a slice of bread, and a tiny packet of jam labeled, 'Manufactured by the Experimental Jam Factory.' I figured they were probably experimenting on us, so I didn't eat it."

I sat down at my desk and glanced at the note that Ken had left for me, explaining what he wanted me to do that day. As usual, the television was on. The anchorman was interviewing a panel of political commentators, all of whom were quick to defend Yeltsin's decision to dissolve Parliament. "Boris Nikolayevich [Yeltsin] is incredibly patient," one of them, a bald man with thick glasses, remarked. "But how much can a person take?" He reminded viewers that for the past two years, the Soviet-era Parliament had blocked the president's reforms at every opportunity. "One can hardly blame him for wanting to get rid of those people," the analyst concluded. Jump-cut to Yeltsin sipping tea in his Kremlin office. Speaking in his stern baritone, Yeltsin put down his teacup and warned that anyone who tried to interfere with the upcoming elections would be arrested immediately. Jump-cut to a press conference inside the White House. "This putsch will collapse with a crash," the Speaker of the House, Ruslan Khasbulatov, declared. Back to Yeltsin again. "What is the next step?" a television journalist asked him. "When do you foresee yourself holding a dialogue with the Supreme

Soviet to work out a compromise?" Yeltsin replied coolly, "There is no Supreme Soviet. Therefore, there is no dialogue, and there can be no dialogue." To cap it all, Rutskoi, the renegade vice president, told the ABC News program *Nightline* that he had appointed his own defense and security ministers, creating a parallel government.

In the United States or Western Europe, such a turn of events would be cause for alarm. But in Russia this kind of political brinkmanship was not unusual. Those early years of reform, from 1991 to 1993, were particularly volatile because the Soviet constitution, which was written for a dictatorship, was still in effect. No one knew how a democratic president or a real legislature was supposed to function. Because there were no rules for the division of power between the executive and legislative branches, president and Parliament clashed constantly. If you turned on the television or radio, you were likely to hear Yeltsin or a member of Parliament say something like, "If we do not reach a compromise, there can be only one outcome: civil war." Each side would use some variation of this line ("Russia will once again be awash in blood, and it will be on your conscience," to quote just one) in an attempt to get the other side to the bargaining table. When you hear such remarks virtually every day, they become like background music: you hardly notice. All of this was just more of the same, I thought, as I watched the news that day.

The fax machine rang, interrupting my musings. I got up and went into the next room to read the latest dispatch: Yeltsin had posted five thousand armed guards around the White House, ostensibly "to prevent bloodshed."

To prevent bloodshed? But such a move would surely *lead* to bloodshed. What if the deputies, as Russian legislators are called, armed themselves too? I pushed the thought out of my mind. Surely the deputies had more sense than that.

A few days later the Russian press reported that the deputies were brandishing pistols and automatic rifles.

Meanwhile Rutskoi—who was now writing decrees on stationery with the words "The President of the Russian Federation" printed on top—ordered Russians to protest against Yeltsin's "dictatorship." Yeltsin fought back with his own brand of spin control. One image was replayed constantly on television: a smiling president taking a stroll through central Moscow and exchanging pleasantries with ordinary Russians. The scene was reminiscent of Yeltsin's days as Moscow Party boss, when he earned a reputation as a man of the people. Unlike other government officials, who preferred to cloister themselves inside the Kremlin's jewelled towers, Yeltsin would show up at a factory, grocery store, or post office, unannounced, just to see how things were going. He would chat with people in his easy, affable way, and they loved him for it.

I knew firsthand how charming the president could be. One morning in 1992 I took a cab to Parliament, but it was snowing so hard that the roads were nearly impassable. By the time I got there, I knew that I had probably missed most of Yeltsin's speech. Hoping to catch at least his concluding remarks, I ran inside. Quickly I took off my coat and boots and handed them to the coatroom attendant. I had just slipped into my high heels and was about to dash into the chamber when I saw Yeltsin, who is usually surrounded by bodyguards, descending the long, red-carpeted staircase by himself. When he reached the bottom—I was standing about ten feet away—he smiled at me and said, "*Zdravstvuytye!* Hello!" I was too stunned to return the greeting, but I was impressed by his warm, friendly manner. He smiled at the coat lady too, and with a gallant little bow he bade her a good morning. The woman, who was perhaps seventy-five, giggled like a teenager. "Hello, hello," she said excitedly. Still starry-eyed, she turned to me and said, "Isn't he wonderful?"

I recalled this episode as I watched Yeltsin walk through the city with prime-time television cameras rolling. The president stopped at Pushkin Square and told a crowd of surprised Muscovites, "We want everything to be peaceful, bloodless. That's our main task." As he spoke, people smiled and gathered around him. He was soon joined by the ministers of Defense and the Interior, General Pavel Grachev and Viktor Yerin. Both men said that their forces were loyal to the only legitimate government: Yeltsin's. Although this display was undoubtedly meant to reassure viewers that the president was still in charge, I, for one, was not convinced. Okay, I thought, so Grachev and Yerin are behind Yeltsin, but what about rank-and-file soldiers?

When the Soviet Union was a superpower, being in the military was a source of pride. Now it could only be described as humiliating, a painful reminder of the country's diminishing power. Thousands of soldiers hadn't been paid in months, and many of those who had been pulled out of Eastern Europe (under Gorbachev) still didn't have a decent place to live. Faced with two presidents, whom would they support? Rutskoi, a decorated hero of the Afghan war who presented himself as sympathetic to the military? Or Yeltsin?

I needed some reassurance, someone to tell me that the situation wasn't as bad as it looked. With the television still blaring in the background, I dialed Svetlana's number.

"*Alyo?*"

"Svetlana, hi. Are you worried?"

"About this latest nonsense, you mean? No, what is there to worry about?"

"How can a country have two presidents? What if people start taking sides?"

"Don't be silly. These political games don't mean a thing. Soon it'll all be over. You'll see."

I was still uneasy, but as the days passed and nothing happened, I convinced myself that Svetlana was probably right: each side would defend its position for another week or so and then a compromise would be found. That was the way it always went. Why should this time be any different?

Ten days after Yeltsin issued his controversial decree, about a hundred deputies and several hundred of their aides and supporters were still holed up inside the White House. Government leaders had tried to persuade them to surrender their weapons, but the talks, which were mediated by Patriarch Aleksy II of the Russian Orthodox Church, collapsed. Every day images of unshaven, exhausted-looking deputies (many had not left the building since the last official session of Parliament) were broadcast on television. Shaking their fists, they looked straight into the camera and spewed invectives at Yeltsin, comparing him to Attila the Hun and even Hitler. "We will not leave this building, even if Yeltsin

comes here with tanks!" one of them raged. Such footage
was always followed by a newscaster's calm assurance that
there had been no violence and that the situation was "normal."

Early one morning, while yet another such scene was
being shown, I was sitting at my desk, sipping coffee and
skimming through the dozens of news dispatches that had
been faxed during the night. One in particular caught my
eye: a list of all the anti-Yeltsin demonstrations scheduled
for that afternoon. By 1993 such demonstrations had become so commonplace that many Western reporters stopped
covering them. After attending the first dozen or so, I, too,
lost interest. The speeches and slogans were always the same.
But the current political crisis seemed like an important
enough reason to go. I felt that we needed to get a sense of
the mood in the city. Ken agreed, and at one o'clock we set
out for Smolenskaya Square in his car. When we arrived, a
military man with a chest full of medals was shouting into a
megaphone, calling for the resurrection of the Soviet Union
and an end to market reforms. The requisite portraits of
Stalin were held high in the air by a few elderly war veterans
dressed in faded military uniforms, an array of colorful medals pinned to their lapels. Every once in a while they cheered
the speaker on with a weak "*Oorah!*" Also in the audience
was a frail, stooped-over woman with a large, hand-written
placard: THE DEMOCRATS HAVE ROBBED THE PEOPLE! The woman
next to her held a picture of Lenin in one hand and a sign
that read: YELTSIN IS A CRIMINAL in the other. They were both
silent.

"I'm hungry," said Ken. "Do you want to get something
to eat?

"Okay."

We got back in the car and drove around until we spotted a small kiosk. PIZZA, read the sign in English. Ken parked the car and we got out to inspect the food in the window: thin slices of Russian bread with watery tomato sauce and *kolbasa* slices.

"Well, it sort of looks like pizza," I said.

"Would you rather go someplace else?"

"We don't have time—the next demonstration starts in twenty minutes. Never mind, I'll survive."

We ordered two of the little pizza look-alikes and some Cokes. There were two white plastic tables but—oddly enough—no chairs. We put our jackets down on one of the tables and ate quickly. Then we drove to October Square to see what was happening there.

In the middle of the square is a colossal statue of Lenin, his fist raised in the air, the lapel of his coat shifting in an imaginary breeze. Although it was October, some of the leaves on the trees were still green. Others had turned orange, yellow, and brown and were crunching beneath our feet. About five hundred people had gathered. I was surprised to see so many young men. Most pro-Communist demonstrations were like the one on Smolenskaya Square— dominated by old people. But something else was amiss here. No one was shouting reactionary slogans or making incendiary speeches. Everyone was just standing there, in silence, as if waiting for some signal. "This is weird," I whispered to Ken. "I wonder what's going on."

By 2:10 the crowd had swelled to about a thousand. The police, who were unarmed, stood on all four corners of the square, their silver riot shields glistening in the midday sun. "There will be no demonstration," one of them said through a bullhorn. "You are requested to disperse and to observe the social order." As he repeated the command, a few people slipped through the cordon the police had formed around the square; the demonstrators whooped and cheered as one small group after another broke through. They must have been as astonished as we were—there was no resistance from the police.

Ken and I followed the crowd to the Garden Ring Road, a major thoroughfare in the center of the city, where more demonstrators were waiting. Standing in the middle of the road, they joined hands and blocked off traffic for several hours before moving on to Krimsky Bridge. The police there seemed to have no idea how to control a crowd either: a column of better-trained Interior Ministry troops marched to the edge of the bridge and stood there, about fifty men against what were now thousands of angry demonstrators. The demonstrators stole their riot shields and truncheons and beat them mercilessly. About five feet away from me, a young man was pummeling a soldier's face with a bloody fist. The soldier fell to the ground. His face was white, and blood was pouring out of his ear; his body was completely still. For a moment I stood there and looked down at him, my eyes wide open in horror, then a voice inside my brain shouted, *Go! Go! Get out of here now!* I ran as fast as I could and hid behind a parapet. Where was Ken? *There* he was, on the other side of the bridge, next to a group of soldiers. They were wiping the blood from their faces with their sleeves. I ran over to him, nearly tripping over a broken bottle.

"Are you all right?" he asked.

"I think so."

Just then someone fired two shots into the air.

"Let's go," Ken said. "Stay close to me. I don't want you getting lost in the crowd."

The mob went on a rampage, smashing the windshield of every bus and car in its path. The streets glittered with broken glass for miles. I had only one thought: What if the mob turns on *us*? These were the kind of people who believed that the CIA had masterminded the breakup of the Soviet Union and installed a puppet regime headed by Yeltsin. They hated Americans. If anyone heard us speaking English . . .

I caught up with Ken, who was a few feet in front of me. *Let's get the hell out of here*, I wanted to say. Instead, keeping my voice down so that no one except Ken could hear me, I said, "Let's think about this for a second. Do you really think we should keep following these people?"

"Absolutely. I want to see where they go."

How could he be so calm? I wondered. But Ken, who was in his mid-forties, was an experienced journalist. He had covered several wars and was probably used to such situations. I was tempted to turn back, but Ken spoke virtually no Russian, and I had agreed to act as his interpreter. I could not abandon him now. We followed the mob all the way to the White House, which was about three miles from October Square. With five thousand soldiers surrounding the building, the place looked like a fortress.

"It would be great if we could talk to Khasbulatov," said Ken, referring to the Speaker of the House.

"*If* he'll talk to us."

"Let's give it a go."

We walked up the steps and showed the uniformed guards our press passes. They waved Ken in, but when I tried to enter the building, one of them said, "Hold it right there. Where do you think you're going?"

"To the fifth floor, to interview Khasbulatov," I replied.

"Women are not allowed inside."

"But he doesn't speak Russian," I said, indicating Ken. "He can't go in there without me."

"What's going on?" Ken asked me. "What's he saying?"

"He won't let me in."

"Why the hell not?"

"Members of the 'weaker sex' are not allowed inside. It's too dangerous. We might get hurt."

Ken rolled his eyes. So much for the interview.

I was used to this sort of treatment. An official at the Foreign Ministry once told me that the woman I had come to see about my visa had gone home for the day. It was a holiday, he explained, and all female employees had a half day. I thought I must have misunderstood him.

"Only the women?" I asked. "But why?"

"This policy is just as it should be," he declared. "Women *are* the weaker sex, after all."

The phrase "weaker sex," which many Russians find charming, is widely used—without a hint of irony. I once heard a television sportscaster announce, "And the weaker sex scored a victory in hockey today. The Russian National Team defeated the German National Team 4 to 3."

In Soviet times women were referred to as "comrades" or even "heroines of socialist labor." Thumb through any current Russian newspaper or magazine and the reason for the change becomes clear: once shown laying down railroad tracks alongside men as part of the latest Five-Year Plan, women are now featured mainly in advertisements, often wearing little more than lipstick. An advertisement for Toshiba, which shows a nude woman holding a laptop computer, is typical. Pornography, illegal under the Communists, is now sold everywhere: in metro stations, on the streets, and in kiosks. But even if one chooses not to buy any of the new publications, it's impossible to escape the barrage of *pornografiya*. Cashiers in shops place one's purchases in plastic bags with pictures of nude women printed on them (one of these, a topless brunette draped in an American flag, is especially popular).

How can women hope to be taken seriously in such an environment?

Even women in positions of power experience their share of humiliation. I was often shocked by the way women were treated in Parliament. "I think we've seen enough beautiful breasts for one day," a male deputy once remarked after two female deputies stepped up to the podium and joined the debate. Derisive hoots of laughter echoed through the chamber. Neither woman ventured to speak again during that session.

But the guard at the top of the stairs didn't care about any of this. And he certainly didn't care whether I interviewed Khasbulatov. As far as he was concerned, my press pass was meaningless. I was a woman, therefore I was not to be admitted inside. End of discussion.

Ken and I went back downstairs and wandered about. Suddenly the surging mob broke through the cordon. Some of the soldiers dropped their machine guns and ran down side streets. A few men with swastikas on their sleeves grabbed the guns and commandeered a convoy of armored personnel carriers. Waving the red flag of the Soviet Union, the men raised the stolen weapons high in the air as they drove off. Crowds of people cheered and chanted, "Soviet Union! Soviet Union!" Someone opened fire, shooting at the crowd; people began screaming and running in all directions. "Get down!" Ken shouted. We dropped to the ground and stayed there. Lying facedown on the cold asphalt, I looked up for a moment and saw two men crouching behind a car. I considered making a dash for it, but the car was too far away. If I run now, I'll be a moving target. I'm better off staying here. More gunfire, louder this time. It was impossible to tell where it was coming from. All I could see was a mass of terrified bodies, scrambling for a place to hide, hundreds of people pushing, shoving, screaming. . . . What was I *doing* here?

When I came back from Georgia a few weeks before, I swore that I would never put myself in such danger again. I had accepted a two-month assignment in Tbilisi, the capital. Although the civil war ended long before I arrived, another war was still going on, so weapons were plentiful. It was not unusual to see someone walking down the street with a grenade launcher or a machine gun. In the entire time that I lived there I never once set my alarm clock. There was no need: I was awakened by the sound of gunfire. The early morning festivities were followed by relative calm. The shooting didn't begin again until after dark, at about seven o'clock in the evening.

One tranquil afternoon I was walking in the warm sunshine when someone fired a gun a few feet above my head. I heard one shot, then another. I looked for a place to run to, but there was nowhere. When I turned around, I saw two dark-skinned men in a rusty orange Pontiac. One of them was brandishing a Kalashnikov assault rifle and laughing hysterically, as though he had just heard some fantastic joke. As he threw his head back, I could see his big white teeth. He fired again. . . . The bullet just missed my right temple. More laughter. My whole body was shaking, my throat was dry, and all I could think of was that I wasn't carrying any identification. When they find my body, they won't even know who I am. My mother will never know what happened to me. Please, God, don't take my life, not yet. I'm only twenty-seven. The men stared at me for a moment, then sped away. As the car made its way up the steep hill, I could hear the roar of the clunky motor and the sound of the man's laughter receding into the distance.

I don't think he meant to kill me; at such close range, he certainly could have. He had misfired deliberately. How amusing it must have been to pull the trigger and watch me cower. "Such things happen," the Georgians I talked to said. "You must learn not to pay any attention."

Not pay any attention? To someone who is aiming a rifle at my head? How was that possible? Perhaps for them it was possible. They were used to such incidents. But for me the constant fear and danger were more than I could bear. I finally decided that no story was worth dying for and returned to Russia, vowing not to do any more war reporting. Thank God I'm back in Moscow, where it's safe, I remember thinking. I tried to get back into my old routine, but I just couldn't: I was worn out. I needed a respite, and what better place to go than New York? My parents were surprised to see me again so soon—I had visited them just six months earlier, for Easter. I never told them what happened in Georgia.

A gentle wind is blowing as I lie on the cold asphalt, my face in my hands. A tense silence. . . . The shooting has subsided. Cautiously I lift my head to see what's going on. The rebels are running down the street. Ken and I get up and run after them. They burst into the mayor's office and drag a man out. The man, who is wearing a suit and tie, has been badly beaten, and his shirt and jacket are torn. "Oh, my God," says Ken. "It's Braginsky." Can that really be Aleksandr Braginsky, the deputy mayor? I take a closer look at the bruised face and see that it is indeed he. The mob begins taunting Braginsky ("Traitor!" "Liar!"), and I'm afraid that they might lynch or shoot him right here; anything seems possible now. But a few people start booing and shouting, "We want Luzhkov! Let's get Luzhkov!" referring to Moscow mayor Yuri Luzhkov. They let the deputy mayor go and surge back into the building. There is the sound of glass crashing as the mob goes from room to room, looking for Luzhkov and shooting wildly. A few young men in green army fatigues climb onto the roof of the mayor's demolished office. When they reach the top, they raise their Kalashnikov rifles in the air. "This is our people's revolution!" one of them, a tall, blond man in a black beret, cries. "I congratulate you, the people!" There is a huge crowd; everyone is shouting, whistling, and waving handkerchiefs. I stare in disbelief as the rebels take down the Russian tricolor flag and raise the old Soviet one, the once reviled ham-

mer and sickle. "The revolution continues!" the man in the
black beret cries, raising his fist toward the blue sky.

"We have triumphed!" someone shouts.

"Death to Yeltsin!"

"All power to the Soviets!"

* * *

Back at the office later that afternoon, Sonia told me that
she and Susan—who was pregnant—were inside the mayor's
office when the rebels stormed the building. Some official
was giving a press conference, and they were standing there,
taking notes. All of a sudden they heard gunfire and the
sound of heavy footsteps. They ran into an empty room and
hid under a conference table, praying that the gunmen would
overlook them. The footsteps paused in front of the door.
They could hear men shouting, arguing. Suddenly the door
swung open. The men burst into the room and opened fire.
Bullets were ricocheting off the top of the table. One of the
gunmen happened to glance underneath and looked straight
at Sonia and Susan. He was so close they could see the color
of his eyes: blue. He cocked the trigger, then turned to his
men and said, "All right, that's it. Let's go."

Why did he spare them? What stopped him from pulling the trigger? Perhaps it was something in their faces.
Maybe he had a wife or a daughter. Or maybe it was because Susan was pregnant. Mothers are revered in Russia.
Perhaps he saw her distended stomach and thought, No, I
can't do it.

Susan had been near hysteria. All she could think about
was her four-year-old daughter, Katy. If I die, what will Katy
do without me? she had thought. I have to get out of here!

She started to get up. But Sonia grabbed her hand and said, "I think we should stay *right here*."

* * *

I poured myself a cup of coffee and turned on the television so that I could watch CNN.

At the top of the screen were the words: SPECIAL REPORT: CRISIS IN RUSSIA.

> The political crisis in Moscow continues. Russian officials say that snipers have been spotted at the Arbat, a popular pedestrian mall near the Kremlin. The men, who are reportedly armed with high-powered rifles equipped with silencers, have been seen on the roofs of some stores.

The camera moved in for a close-up of the *Irlansky Dom na Arbatye*—my grocery store. It can't be, I thought. How can there be snipers on the roof of my grocery store?

Ken came over to me. "I need you to talk to some of the government troops. Find out what their orders are."

"Where should I go?"

"Check the Arbat. There should be some tanks there. But be careful. There have been reports—"

"Of snipers. I know."

"Don't take any unnecessary risks."

If I hadn't been so exhausted, I might have laughed. What could he mean? Didn't going to a sniper zone qualify as an "unnecessary risk?" What kind of crazy profession was this?

Trying not to sound sarcastic, I said, "Don't worry, I'll be careful. I'll be back as soon as I can."

As I walked through the Arbat that afternoon, it was hard to believe that the country was on the edge of civil war. Mothers were walking with young children, smiling and eating ice cream. Vendors were doing a brisk business selling fresh flowers, popcorn, and the usual menagerie of souvenirs: Soviet military hats and uniforms, matrioshka dolls, hand-painted jewelry, and lacquered boxes. The department stores were crowded too. What were all these people doing here? How could anyone even think of buying roses or trying on a sweater in a boutique at such an hour?

The wind was blowing through the trees. A single yellow leaf floated slowly to the ground. A gray squirrel was poised on a branch. It scurried to the ground, picked up an acorn with its paws, and began devouring it, making a crunching sound. When it saw me, it dropped the acorn and scampered away. There was my grocery store. I looked up at the roof. Were there really snipers there? It seemed so impossible. I didn't see anyone, but no sniper worth his mettle would let his victim see him. Snipers shoot from windows where there is only a pale blue curtain fluttering in the breeze, from deserted rooftops where there are only birds singing.

With my bright purple jacket, I knew that I was an easy target. I imagined a man in a black ski mask holding an automatic rifle and looking at me through the crosshairs of his scope. Maybe I should take the jacket off. But it was cold. Why hadn't I thought to wear something less conspicuous? As I neared the end of the sniper zone, my heart beat loudly, and I could feel the sweat pouring down my back. At last I spotted five tanks and about twenty soldiers. A few were leaning against the massive tanks, smoking cigarettes, their green camouflage caps half covering their eyes. I asked one of them what his orders were. What was the Defense Ministry's plan? He screwed up his blue eyes and stared at me.

"What are you doing here?" he sneered. "Why don't you go home and cook dinner for your husband?"

"I'm a journalist," I said. "I'm supposed to be here. Why don't you just let me do my job, and I'll let you do yours."

He lit another cigarette. "I don't think they really have a plan," he said, pointing in the direction of the Kremlin with his thumb. "For now our orders are just to stay here. Anything else you want to know?"

When I got back to the office, I photocopied my notes and left them on Ken's desk. I needed a break. I poured myself another cup of coffee and called Svetlana.

"How's it going?" I asked.

"Not bad," she answered. "I baked an apple pie this morning for Irina, the one who was going for her doctorate in chemistry. I think you met her once."

"No, I don't think so."

"Well, anyhow, she finally finished her dissertation a couple of months ago and her defense was today. I promised her that I would bake an apple pie and that we would celebrate the day she got her degree, so I took the pie over to MGU [Moscow State University]."

"You went all the way to MGU? Today?"

"Yeah, I saw a few tanks," she said matter-of-factly. "I know what you're thinking—I must be crazy. But she worked so *hard* and I promised her years ago. I just couldn't let her down."

"So how did the defense go?"

"She said they asked her a lot of questions and that she was kind of nervous. But she managed to answer all of them, and they gave her the Ph.D. She looked so happy when she came out. The pie was still warm—I wrapped it up really well—We went to her office and ate the whole thing."

"Well, you certainly are original," I teased, repeating a Russian expression that Svetlana often used when I did something that struck her as odd. "Traveling around the city in the middle of all this."

"What am I supposed to do? Don't you realize that this could go on for months or even, God forbid, years?"

I didn't know how to answer her. It was true, of course, what she said—no one knew how long this was going to last. And what *were* people supposed to do in the meantime?

After I hung up I thought about Svetlana, Irina, the dissertation committee, and all the people I had seen at the Arbat that afternoon, calmly going about their everyday lives, and I realized that they were not crazy or even especially brave. It occurred to me that people try to behave as normally as possible during war (or the threat of war) because going about your daily routine is an excellent way of denying the danger all around you. Irina and the members of the dissertation committee could have stayed home all day, nervously listening to the latest news reports. Svetlana and the Arbat shoppers could have stayed home too, watching and waiting. But how long were they supposed to wait?

I had the kind of headache I always get when I am under extreme stress—a sharp pain just above the eyes. I wanted only one thing: to take some aspirin and lie down in a dark room. But it was time to get back to work. I turned on the

TV (to the Russian State Channel) and grabbed a yellow legal pad so that I could take notes. As the announcer began reading the news, I could hear the sound of gunfire in the studio. About twenty minutes into the broadcast, there was a loud noise that sounded like an explosion. "It's hard to talk," the announcer said nervously, "the conflict between Russians has reached its limits—" And the screen went blank.

By early evening all channels featured only a blank screen or cartoons. It turned out that the sound I heard *was* an explosion. As we later learned from watching CNN, one of the rebels had blasted open the television station's front door with a rocket-propelled grenade as the announcer was reading the news. The rebels insisted that their action was justified because Ostankino, the main television tower from which all news is broadcast, was pro-Yeltsin and had denied them their fair share of air-time.

By nightfall we could hear gunshots outside, and Ken warned us not to stand by the window. Shaky radio announcers read updates on the situation that became more frightening by the hour: "The Government of the Russian Federation has issued a warning: Do not go outside. Do not let your children outside. All citizens are ordered to *stay indoors* until further notice." And then:

> The fighting inside Ostankino continues. . . . Groups of men armed with clubs, iron bars, and guns, who are thought to be supporters of the legislature, have been spotted around the city. Eyewitnesses report that they are waving both the Soviet flag and the czarist one. The bandits have already killed twenty-five

people, including children. Hundreds have been wounded.

I had two stories to file: one for *Newsday* and one for the *Boston Herald*. The first was due in New York by 11 P.M. The second had to be ready by midnight. It was already nine o'clock. But my headache had worsened—it now felt like someone was smashing cymbals together inside my head—and I could not concentrate.

I got up to check the fax. The latest report said that the insurgents were preparing to take over the Kremlin. I passed this bit of news on to Ken, who was busy watching CNN and writing his own story. Turning toward me, he took off his glasses, and I noticed that his eyes, like mine, were red from lack of sleep. (We were all working eighteen-hour days.) "Do me a favor?" he said. "Make me a copy of that report? Thanks. Oh, there's a fax for you. It came this morning." He handed me a large brown envelope. "When you're done with your stories, go to my place and fix yourself something to eat. Here's the key." I put the key in my pocket and went into the next room to photocopy the report. After I gave it to Ken, I went back to my desk and opened the envelope. The fax was written in Ukrainian, in my mother's small, elegant hand. It was signed "*Mishka*," my nickname for her, which means "little mouse" in Ukrainian. My mother . . . What must she be thinking right now? I recalled the look in her eyes when I first told her that I intended to go to Russia. She recoiled from me, as though I had just slapped her. I remembered the pain and anger in her voice. "What if there's another revolution? Do you want to die young?" But most of all, I remembered her tears. For three whole days she cried. And yet she accepted my decision, accepted my assurances that everything would be all right—or pretended to. What could I say to her now? Would she ever forgive me?

I skimmed the letter and stuffed it into my backpack. After I finished both stories, I put on my jacket and walked to Ken's apartment, which was in the building next door. Sonia, who was in the kitchen, looked up when I opened the door.

"How are you holding up?" she asked as she added some mayonnaise to the tuna fish she had put in a bowl.

"Okay, I guess," I said, lying.

"What if this turns into a full-blown civil war? What are we gonna do?"

"I don't know," I said, taking some cold cuts and a jar of pickles out of the refrigerator. "I've been trying not to think about that."

"If it gets worse, I'm going back to New York. Everyone always makes it sound so noble when reporters are killed during something like this, but it's not like we're doctors or something. I mean, what are we risking our lives for? To get a story into the paper? So we can see our names in print? There's nothing noble about it. It's totally self-centered."

"You're right," I said softly. "It's not worth it."

I sat down at the table and made myself a ham-and-cheese sandwich.

"I'd better get back to the office," Sonia said.

"You didn't finish your story?"

"I did, but Ken might need me to translate something. See ya later."

She closed the door quietly, leaving me alone with my thoughts. What if the Communists came to power again? They would almost certainly bar people from leaving the country. I thought about my relatives, the ones who perished under Stalin. Like them, I had come to the Soviet Union voluntarily. I had assumed, as they did, that I would be free to leave whenever I chose. Maybe I should leave *now*, while I still have the chance. I'll go to the airport tomorrow morning and buy a ticket for the next flight to New York. Ken will understand. I'll go back to the office and tell him right now. Then I remembered that my visa had expired. I forgot to renew it. What if I leave and the crisis ends next week? With no visa, I won't be able to get back into the country. Do I want to leave? What about my work? My friends? My apartment? How can I just abandon everything?

Although the windows were closed, I could hear the wind moving restlessly through the trees, ripping leaves from their branches. I went into the living room. On the coffee table was a notebook. I tore out a sheet of paper and wrote a note to my mother.

Dear Mishka,

Just got your letter a few hours ago. To answer some of your questions, yes, I have enough food and I'm perfectly healthy, a little tired, but nothing more than that, so please don't worry. I'm sorry that this is so short. I'll write you a real letter when all this is over.

Love always,
Lori

It was one o'clock in the morning, and I was getting tired. I would fax the note to Yonkers tomorrow. Although I could not imagine my old-world parents, who are uncomfortable with any kind of technology, using a fax machine, they have one in their bedroom. Knowing that the Russian postal service is unreliable, they bought it for only one reason: so that they could communicate with me.

Given the circumstances, Ken and Susan suggested that Sonia and I spend the night at their apartment. Sonia would stay in the guest room. I was to sleep on the sofa bed in the living room. Susan gave me an oversize T-shirt. I put it on, took a couple of aspirin, and climbed into bed. I was lying there, under a warm quilt, trying to fall asleep, when I heard the patter of little feet on the soft carpet. I opened my eyes. It was Katy. She was wearing white cotton pajamas with tiny pink-and-blue bunny rabbits. Her short blond hair was slightly tousled. Her large blue eyes, with their long lashes, looked even larger in the dark.

"Hi, sweetheart."

She looked down at her pajamaed feet, smiling shyly. "Lori, can I brush your hair?"

"Sure."

"Yeah!"

I reached for my backpack, took out my hairbrush and handed it to Katy. It looked so big in her small hand.

"Turn around," she commanded.

She climbed into bed with me and began brushing my hair, using rough, awkward strokes.

"Like this," I told her, running the brush through her fine hair. "Gently, slowly."

She tried again, a little less rough this time.

"*That's* it," I told her. "Now you've got it."

She put the brush on the end table and jumped back into bed, pulling the quilt up to her chin. "Night night."

"Night night."

Katy's head was touching my shoulder, and I could smell the fresh baby scent of her skin. She nestled closer to me and for a few moments, as I listened to her breathing softly, I forgot that outside a revolution was unfolding.

When I awoke the next morning, there was a small space where Katy had been. Where could she have gone? Back to her own room, probably. I tiptoed down the hall and opened her door. There she was, with her teddy bear under one arm, still asleep. Poor thing, I thought, she must be exhausted after being up so late. I went back into the living room, drew the curtains, and looked out the window. The sun was shining, and tanks were rolling through the streets. Were these Yeltsin's troops or pro-Parliament militants? There was no way to distinguish one side from the other.

I took a quick shower, put on my jacket, and ran to the office. Ken was already at his desk, reading the latest fax reports. Wordlessly he handed me the most recent dispatch, which was still warm from the fax machine. Quickly I skimmed it. At 6:45 that morning Yeltsin representatives had held negotiations with envoys from Parliament, but the two sides had failed to reach an agreement. Lieutenant General Aleksandr Kulikov, who was appointed commandant in charge of the state of emergency in Moscow, had given the rebels and their supporters an ultimatum: if they did not surrender, they would be "eliminated." Ken and I looked at each other: this was it. Yeltsin was bringing in the army.

By 8:30 A.M., government tanks were firing huge shells at the White House. Sonia turned on the television in Ken's apartment—the attack was being covered live by CNN, which had been picked up by Russian channels. We watched as the first shell, which exploded in a great cloud of black smoke, destroyed Khasbulatov's fifth-floor office. Specially-trained paratroopers burst into the charred building and fought with rebels inside, while three government helicopters circled overhead, monitoring snipers on the roof. The rebels fought back with a steady stream of automatic gunfire. Just after noon a military commander in green-and-brown camouflage called out through a bullhorn, "People in the White House. Give yourselves up while you still have a chance." The rebels continued to fire.

By this time several floors of the building were ablaze, and there were huge holes where once rows of offices had been. Hundreds of curious onlookers scrambled to get a better view. A few teenagers climbed trees; others sat on their friends' shoulders, as though they were at a rock concert. I sat on the edge of the couch, trying to absorb what was happening on the screen in front of me. Was it possible that I was actually watching live television coverage of people killing one another?

Every so often one of the spectators would fall, wounded—or dead. The doctors who examined them said that the majority of those who were killed had been shot in the head, probably by snipers. Why were these people allowed to stay? Why didn't the army clear the area?

At 2:30 P.M. three men waving white flags came out of the burning building. "Bring us Rutskoi!" the crowd shouted. A few hours later hundreds of rebels gave themselves up. As they walked out into the sunshine, with their hands behind their heads, the crowd again demanded Rutskoi. The vice president had vowed "to fight until the last cartridge," but at 6:00 P.M., both he and Khasbulatov surrendered. By nightfall dozens of bloody corpses lined the front of the White House, and about three hundred rebels were still inside.

After it was all over, Yeltsin gave a televised speech. Looking grave and at times tearful, he said, "It is not necessary to say that someone won and someone lost. Today such words would be inappropriate. People died—our brothers—and we cannot bring them back. This is our common tragedy, our common pain. . . . [T]he most frightening events are behind us." But, he said, "If anyone thinks that the situation has been completely normalized, this is a big mistake. Passions have not been quieted." Parliament supporters and special police units were still waging sporadic gun battles; some of the people suspected of leading the attacks on the mayor's office and television tower had not been caught yet; and snipers remained in some neighborhoods.

Nevertheless, the main battle had ended, and Ken said that I could go home. My assignment was over.

It felt good to be in my own kitchen again. I ate some boiled cabbage and rice (everything else had spoiled), and after washing the dishes, I took a shower and went to bed. When I woke up and looked at the clock, I was stunned. It was half past noon. I had slept for nearly fourteen hours.

I don't know how to explain what I felt then. The mind reaches a point, I think, when it cannot absorb any more. In those first few days, as I bought food, did the laundry, and cleaned my apartment, I still couldn't believe that it had come to this: 150 dead, including an American lawyer who happened to be at the television station; and six hundred wounded, six of them Americans (four were journalists). (In the 1991 coup, three people were killed.)

One morning I went to the Foreign Ministry to renew my visa. On the way home, I walked past Krimsky Bridge. I remembered the soldier's white face. The blood coming out of his ear. His body sprawled out on the ground . . . "He's dead!" I said aloud. A couple of old women who were sitting on the side of the bridge, selling vegetables, turned around and stared at me. Dark, rain-filled clouds were moving in the sky. . . . A flock of birds was flying past a row of buildings. . . . There was no blood on the road. Someone must have washed it away. Everything looked just as it always did, except that there were hardly any cars. The clouds were moving again. . . . It started to rain, and I walked slowly back to my apartment.

The fax my mother sent was still on my desk. Remembering my promise to her, I sat down and wrote this letter:

October 10, 1993

Dear Mishka,

Here's the "real" letter I promised to write you. Things have calmed down, but the crisis isn't over yet. There are still a few tanks by the White House, and soldiers armed with machine guns are patrolling the streets. The state of emergency has been extended until October 18, which means that there is an 11:00 P.M. curfew. It's a real pain if you want to go out at night. Last Wednesday I went out for coffee with Svetlana, and we were having so much fun that we lost all track of the time. When we got to the metro, it was already 10:20. I just made it—I got back to my apartment at 10:56. I'll have to be more careful.

As far as the government is concerned, there is only one valid reason to be out after eleven o'clock: if you work at night. And even then you have to get a special pass that shows you have permission to be out past curfew. If a policeman or soldier asks to see your pass and you don't have one, you'll be taken to the nearest police station. (So far 3,800 people have been arrested.) The worst part is that you have to spend at least three days in jail while the police investigate the reason you violated the curfew.

One good thing has come out of all of this: crime has gone way down because of all the troops in the streets. I feel a lot safer than I did three weeks ago.

Life is slowly getting back to normal. Today I even went to the Arbat to do my grocery shopping. Don't worry, I only went after I heard on the radio that the area had been "cleansed" of snipers.

It's almost two o'clock in the morning. I should be in bed, but I've been having trouble sleeping lately. I'd like to come home for a visit sometime soon. I think I need to get away for a while.

All my love,
Lori

A few weeks later my mother ran into a friend of hers, an old Ukrainian woman whom she hadn't seen in a long time. The woman, who had known me since I was a child, happened to see footage of the Krimsky Bridge riot on satellite television.

"I was watching all that violence over there," she told my mother, "and in the middle of all those demonstrators, there was this girl running around with a notebook. When I took a closer look, I said to myself, 'Why, that looks just like Piotr Cidylo's younger daughter. But it can't be. What would she be doing in Moscow, in the middle of a coup?'"

"Now the older one," she remarked, referring to my sister, "*her* I can imagine doing something like that, but not Lori. She was always so quiet and studious. I always thought she should become a librarian. What is she doing these days?"

"Actually . . ." my mother began.

Acknowledgments

MANY PEOPLE HELPED bring this book to fruition. I would like to thank my editors at *Newsday*, *The Economist*, the *Chicago Tribune*, the *Miami Herald*, the *Financial Times*, and the *Daily News* for giving me the opportunity to write about Russia. Special thanks go to Mike Pingree, the foreign editor of the *Boston Herald*, for supporting my visa for five years and for providing humor and encouragement during tumultuous times in Moscow. I am also grateful to Anita and Jordan Miller, my editors at Academy Chicago, who rescued this book from oblivion; to my friends Karin, Susan, Elizabeth, and Barbara, and my brother, Peter, for their unwavering support; and to Olya, who first suggested this book.

Most of all I would like to thank all my Russian friends, many of whom appear in these pages, for sharing their lives and the wonders of Russia with me.